"*Taming the Spirited Child* reminds us of the importance of always working to strike the right balance—which is different for each and every child—between empathy, love, expectation, and limits as we go about our work as parents and teachers."
—WILLIAM S. PEEBLES, IV, Headmaster,
The Lovett School, Atlanta, Georgia

"A wonderful, heartwarming book for any parent who has ever wanted to throw up her hands in despair over her child's repeated misbehavior. This book not only gives them hope; it gives them answers!"
—BETTIE B. YOUNGS, author,
Taste Berries for Teens

"This is a book that needed to be written! Dr. Michael Popkin has done a wonderful job in providing a resource that will help those millions of parents of spirited children live happier, more satisfying family lives while giving their children the gift of love and limits."
—ROBYN FREEDMAN SPIZMAN, author,
The Thank You Book

ALSO BY MICHAEL H. POPKIN

PARENTING PROGRAMS

(full curriculums that include a parent guide, leader's guide, and video)

Active Parenting Now: For Parents of Children Ages 5 to 12

Active Parenting of Teens

1, 2, 3, 4 Parents! Parenting Children Ages 1-to-4 (with Marilyn Montgomery and Betsy Gard)

Parents on Board: Building Academic Success Through Parent Involvement (with Bettie B. Youngs and Jane M. Healy)

Free the Horses: A Self-Esteem Adventure (with Susan D. Greathead)

Active Teaching: Enhancing Discipline, Self-Esteem and Student Performance

Windows: Healing and Helping Through Loss (with Mary J. Hannaford)

BOOKS

DocPop's 52 Weeks of Active Parenting

Getting Through to Your Kids (with Robyn Freedman Spitzer)

Active Parenting: Teaching Cooperation, Courage, and Responsibility

Quality Parenting (with Linda Albert)

So . . . Why Aren't You Perfect Yet?

For more information about these and other resources or to find a parenting class near you go to: www.activeparenting.com.

TAMING

— the —

SPIRITED CHILD

Strategies for Parenting
Challenging Children Without
Breaking Their Spirits

MICHAEL H. POPKIN, PH.D.

A Fireside Book
PUBLISHED BY SIMON & SCHUSTER
New York   London   Toronto   Sydney

FIRESIDE
Rockefeller Center
1230 Avenue of the Americas
New York, NY 10020

FIRESIDE and colophon are registered trademarks of Simon & Schuster, Inc.

For information regarding special discounts for bulk purchases, please contact Simon & Schuster Special Sales at 1-800-456-6798 or business@simonandschuster.com.

Designed by Mary Austin Speaker

Manufactured in the United States of America

10 9 8 7 6 5 4 3 2 1

ISBN-13: 978-0-7432-8689-3
ISBN-10:   0-7432-8689-8

To my wife, Melody, my parenting partner,
and our children, Megan and Ben

Contents

CONTENTS

TAMING

— the —

SPIRITED CHILD

Introduction

"I am so unhappy. I cannot play with you," the fox said. "I am not tamed."

"Ah! Please excuse me," said the little prince. But, after some thought, he added: "What does that mean, 'tame'?"

"It is an act too often neglected," said the fox. "It means to establish ties . . . To me, you are still nothing more than a little boy like a hundred thousand other little boys. And I have no need of you. And you, on your part, have no need of me. To you, I am nothing more than a fox like a hundred thousand other foxes. But if you tame me, then we shall need each other. To me, you shall be unique in all the world. To you, I shall be unique in all the world."

—THE LITTLE PRINCE,
by Antoine de Saint-Exupéry

THE RELATIONSHIP BETWEEN parent and child is, ideally, one characterized by a special bond of love in which each person is unique and special in all the world to the other. Unfortunately, in my thirty years of working with parents and children, I have found anger; fighting and resentment too often characterize this relationship, with each person attempting to exercise his or her will over the other. These classic power struggles are present from time to time in almost all families and occur with disturbing frequency in more families than ever before. In one survey of parents enrolled in a six-session course for parents of elementary-age children, 75 percent said they were there because of such power struggles.

During three recent guest appearances on *The Montel Williams Show*, I was asked to evaluate and offer advice to a number of families that were having trouble with their children. In each case a power struggle was evident; but what was unique about these children was their sensitivity to outside triggers (whether it was a parental request or a scratchy shirt) and the intensity of their reactions. For example, one two-year-old child had already been having a violent tantrum for over an hour when Montel's audience saw his expression of rage at his father for trying to get him to take off his shirt before taking a bath. It was a difficult scene to watch, but it was painfully familiar to many members of the audience. Tantrums that last for hours over seemingly inconsequential matters seem to have become part of the everyday experience of many families.

In recent years, such tantrum-prone kids have been labeled "difficult," "strong-willed," and "defiant." More recent, they have also been called "quirky" and even "spirited." They are often intense, hypersensitive, persistent, distractible, and unwilling to accept change. But—like the spirited horse Seabiscuit, in the book and movie of the same name—once tamed, they can not only become successful, but champions.

While the term *taming* may suggest whips and chains to some, the real key to taming a spirited child is to establish a relationship. This is the taming that the fox spoke of to the Little Prince in Antoine de Saint-Exupéry's classic children's story. When coupled with effective methods of discipline, communication, and encouragement, relationship-building skills can be used to help a child learn to live more effectively in the family and in the world. As one mother put it after learning these skills and experiencing a positive change in her spirited son, "The best part to me was the reawakening of the feeling of joy for my child."

Do You Have a Spirited Child?

I would rather be ashes than dust! I would rather that my spark
should burn out in a brilliant blaze than it should be stifled by
dry rot. I would rather be a superb meteor, every atom of me in
magnificent glow, than a sleepy and permanent planet. The proper
function of man is to live, not to exist. I shall not waste my days
in trying to prolong them. I shall use my time.
                                    —JACK LONDON (1876–1916)

JACK LONDON, A talented and popular writer of adventure tales,
including *Call of the Wild,* the story of a sled dog in Alaska, spent his
adult life writing, championing social causes, and struggling for peace
of mind. London was probably once a spirited child, the kind of child
that prompted the late humorist Sam Levenson to quip that "insanity
is hereditary—you get it from your children." If you have a child
who is driving you crazy, chances are that you are grimacing rather
than laughing right now. I'll also wager that you find yourself angry
a lot. You may feel like one mother who confided to me recently, "I
never even knew I *could* get angry until I had Alex!" Some kids just
seem to know how to push our buttons in ways we never dreamed
possible.

Such kids have been called by many different names over the
years—and to be sure, they are not all alike. They used to be simply referred to as "defiant" or "rebellious." Later, books were written about "the problem child," "the strong-willed child," and "the

difficult child." They are often described as impulsive, hyperactive, aggressive, noncompliant, difficult to manage, ornery, temperamental, oppositional, or just "all boy." Some kids even get diagnostic labels such as ADHD (attention deficit/hyperactivity disorder), obsessive-compulsive, bipolar, and so on. Sometimes these labels are useful for knowing what, if any, medication might be prescribed to help a child. I'm not here to engage in label bashing because, when medication can help, I'm all for getting that help to children and their parents. I'm also not suggesting that all of these children are the same. There are often important differences between children diagnosed one way or another, differences that affect the choice of treatment.

But often labels are merely arbitrary handles that writers and mental health professionals use as shortcuts for fuller descriptions of behaviors that they think get in the way of a child's successful functioning in society. We also know that such judgments are specific to our time and place in history. A hyperaggressive child might have been highly functional in a war-making society in the Dark Ages, for example, but in this century he will likely wind up in the principal's office, the boss's office, and the warden's office unless he changes his ways. Jack London, though one of the most talented and successful writers of his time, suffered from alcoholism and depression, and died at the young age of forty an unhappy man, his spirited nature never successfully tamed.

Changing the Child's Ways, Not the Child's Being

The one thing that all of these labels have in common is that they are negative. *Defiant, problem, rebellious, strong willed,* and the like all smack of an underlying condition that needs to be healed. They suggest that there is something abnormal about the child at a very deep level. Something seems to have gone terribly wrong in the child, and it must be remedied. Once this is understood, the theory goes, it can be treated; and once treated, the child can be returned to normalcy. This will ensure that he no longer spends time in the principal's office, the boss's office, or the warden's office. Instead he will function as a contributing member of society, pay his taxes on time, and contribute to a growing gross national product.

This pathology-based approach is not always all bad. A lot of kids and their parents have been helped by it, and many more will be helped by it. The problem, however, is that by dwelling on a presumed underlying problem, we can miss the real strengths these nonconformist kids bring to the table, the gifts that characterize spirited children. They are not pathological at their core. Most have a fire and energy at their core that, if harnessed, might fuel a lifetime of great achievement. While their particular ways of expressing this energy is often out of sync with the times in which they live, the power within them should be a source of inspiration for the rest of us. Certainly they may need to redirect their gifts, so that they do not become the unwanted warriors in a time of peace, the unacknowledged iconoclasts in an age of conformity, or the untamed thoroughbreds never invited to the Kentucky Derby. Which brings me to the following analogy.

Seabiscuit Rides Again

The movie and book *Seabiscuit* stole the hearts of the public in 2003. In 1938, the underdog horse upon which the story was based became the champion by defeating the legendary War Admiral by four lengths. Seabiscuit became a hero during a period of American history, the Depression, when people needed to believe that the little guy could succeed in spite of overwhelming odds. Seabiscuit, a small horse with a huge spirit, came to the rescue of a nation.

Of course, if you saw the movie, you'll remember that Seabiscuit wasn't always a champion. In fact, he was actually an untamed, out-of-control terror that was almost put to sleep because he caused so much chaos. Fortunately, a wealthy owner saw promise in Seabiscuit's rebelliousness and bought him, saving the future champion from a bullet. There is a powerful scene in which five or six handlers try to rein in Seabiscuit, while he struggles mightily against their attempts to harness him. They are losing the battle and ready to give up when a young red-headed jockey (the story's other hero), who has a partially untamed spirit of his own, also sees something special in this defiant, strong-willed, difficult to manage, *magnificent* horse. The talented and caring jockey is able to win Seabiscuit's trust, tame him, and help realize the championship potential with which this spirited horse was born.

It is obvious where I am going with this, right? Inside many spirited children are champions who need the taming of firm and loving parents, or surrogate parents, to bring out their best and perhaps save them from self-destruction. Without such taming, the lives of these kids can go further and further wrong, often ending up in one form of confinement or another. In and out of time-out as children, they resign themselves early to being at odds with any form of authority. As teens, their spirited behavior gets them into more and more trouble—sometimes landing them in jail, a hospital, a psychiatric unit or worse.

Taming, Not Breaking

Some parents mistakenly believe that they need to break the will of a spirited child, even punishing him into obedience, like a horse trainer who beats a horse until the animal breaks. This was *not* how Seabiscuit was tamed, and it's not about to work with most spirited kids. The problem with the heavy-handed approach is that spirited children have a keen sense of respect and disrespect. When parents rely on punishment, especially harsh punishment, to break the child's will, the child feels trampled on and becomes resentful. Since these kids are anything but passive, they do not take such perceived injustices lying down. They rear up like Seabiscuit and rebel. Some of these kids can rebel very well and very long, which accounts for that feeling of anger on the part of the parent that I acknowledged in the opening paragraph. Parents who try to break such children are in for the fight of their lives—often becoming frustrated and angry, if not thoroughly defeated. I'll talk more about these kinds of power struggles, and about methods to avoid them, later in the book. I'll also teach you methods for taming spirited children that are much more respectful of you as a parent and your child as a person, as well as more successful.

Some parents are thinking right now that they know of at least one child who has been successfully broken by a strong-willed parent who used a lot of harsh discipline. There are even well-known child experts, whose books suggest breaking the child's will through punishment. But even if you could use sufficient force to break the child, here's my question: Why would you *want* a broken child when, with a different approach, you could have a whole child who behaves well? I speak from experience, as well as from my professional training. Our son, Benjamin, was a spirited child. He would throw the most impressive tantrums, the reverberations from which may have registered on a Richter scale someplace. He had his own mind, and he wanted what he wanted when he wanted it. By the time he was four, we knew it was time to intervene. Oh, he was also charming, happy, funny, smart, and otherwise a joy to be around. Our job as parents was not to break him, and risk losing all of these positive gifts, but rather to tame him so that he learned to use his gifts in positive ways.

For years I had been teaching other parents strategies for raising challenging, powerful children. I had worked with hundreds of frustrated parents in therapy sessions, and over two million parents had completed my *Active Parenting* courses, six-session video-based groups that teach a complete approach to parenting. Many had taken time to write about how well these methods worked, not only to change their children's lives but to improve their own lives as well. We had some twenty different studies showing the effectiveness of these methods and thousands of parent educators who endorsed and used our programs.

But now it was time to practice with our own spirited child what I had preached. The shoe was on the other foot, and at times it pinched. My wife and I found that though these strategies worked, they required a patience and awareness not as necessary as when parenting our other, quite-different child. I'll share these strategies in detail in this book, strategies that I know work from firsthand experience. It may have taken us a little longer to see a change in our son, but it was worth it; by age six his tantrums and other misbehaviors were well behind him. He's now a thriving teenager who lives within the rules and shows his spirit productively while enjoying life fully.

Nature, Nurture, Genes, and Parenting

There was a time in the not-so-distant past when many psychologists thought that children came into the world as blank slates, to be written upon by their environment. In other words, their personalities were shaped almost entirely by parents, teachers, and other agents of society. Genes were given credit for eye color and other physical attributes, but not much for intelligence, personality, and behavior. If you had a spirited child (by any name), then you could be sure, according to the blank-slate theory, that somebody had turned the child that way. That "somebody" was usually the parent, who inevitably got a lot of the blame for the child's robust behavior and misbehavior.

Numerous studies, using the handy circumstance of genetic twins who were separated at birth and raised in different environments, pointed out the overwhelming fallacy of the blank-slate theory. So many of these twins were so much alike in their behavior and personalities, in spite of vastly different upbringings, that even the most nurture-oriented of those in the field of psychology had to admit that much of who we are as individuals seems to have been genetically programmed. Parents and other forces in a child's upbringing, to be sure, do play important roles in determining what choices the child makes regarding these inherited genetic traits—whether he becomes Batman or the Joker, for example. But the basic cards have been dealt.

This is a good news–bad news proposition. The good news is that you probably aren't to blame for your child's spirited disposition. That was in all likelihood part of the hand he (and you) were dealt in the great genetic poker game. The bad news is that you aren't entirely off the hook, either. You and other forces in your child's environment (his siblings, teachers, other adults, life experiences, what he reads or sees or listens to—all that and more) do play a huge role in either taming your spirited child so that he uses his unique gifts for the common good *or* influencing him to become more defiant, rebellious, and out of control, until he eventually does damage to himself and others, winding up in trouble, in jail, or in the morgue. Throughout history, some spirited children have become great leaders, or at least contributing members of society, while others have become dastardly villains, or at least obnoxious neighbors. And their parents probably did play an important role in determining which road they eventually traveled.

They just may not have played as conscious a role as you are going to after you finish reading this book.

Traits of the Spirited Child (CAPPS)

When I was a young and spirited child, I used to have a cap pistol. And like a lot of boys of my generation, I'd run around the yard playing cowboy and making loud noises by shooting off my caps. This was a lot of fun until the day I brought the gun inside and woke up my baby sister while chasing imaginary bank robbers through the house. My parents were not amused.

While every child is unique in his own way, spirited children do share some commonalties. They tend to be extra Curious, Adventurous, Powerful, Persistent, and Sensitive. CAPPS—like capital letters they tend to be bigger than life; like my childhood cap gun, explosive, full out, and energetic. See how many of these traits apply to your child. The more they have and the more often they exhibit them, the more likely that you are the proud parent of a spirited child.

Spirited Children Are More Curious

Tania (age eleven) was described by her mother as a royal pain to take shopping. "We could never get out of there," she complained. "Tania was always seeing something else that she wanted to look at. I'd be ready to check out, only to turn around and find her across the store, looking at something else."

Peter (age seven) was hardly ever able to get himself dressed and downstairs for breakfast on time. Something would always catch his attention and distract him along the way.

Whatever George (age nine) was thinking about at the time, he was absolutely absorbed in it—to such a degree that his parents would have to call his name two or three times before they could get his attention. They complained in frustration that "he never seems to be listening."

George, like many spirited kids, *was* listening. He was listening to his own mind explore the curiosities of the world in which he lived. Spirited kids often get so fixated on something of interest to them— like a dog, a crack in the cement, or how high a ball can bounce when dropped out of the second-story window—that any distraction will be unheard or ignored. It doesn't seem to matter whether the object of their attention is right there in front of them or only in their mind's eye. Their curiosity and focus can be profound. This may drive parents and others trying to break through to them crazy, but the upside is that spirited kids often use their heightened curiosity to make great contributions later in life. I'd bet that Benjamin Franklin and Henry Ford were spirited children.

Spirited Children Are More Adventurous

Wanda (age five) would get up early in the morning and go exploring downstairs while her parents and siblings still slept. One morning her mother came down to find Wanda sitting amid a box of Pop-Tarts, which she had spread creatively across the floor in a life-size mural.

Jonathon (age seven) was, in his mother's words, "without fear. He was the type of kid who will always leap before he looks." Consequently, Jonathon spent many an hour getting stitched and mended in emergency rooms when his leaping came to unfortunate ends.

Jerry (age twenty) dropped out of college after his second year to travel the country in his van. He figured that "there was just too much of life out there that I was missing sitting in the classroom day after day."

It isn't that any of these children are bad or malicious. Rather, they have been given a temperament that makes them want to experience life in as big a way as possible. They yearn for adventure. Like Jack London, they want to journey to distant lands, to zip across the cosmos like a "superb meteor." Like Pablo Picasso, they want to create something new and different—and if the nose ends up on the side of the head instead of in the middle of the face, so much the better! Like Amelia Earhart, the first woman of aviation, they seek to go where no one has gone before. Of course, this inevitably brings them into conflict with parents, siblings, teachers, and others who live within the boundaries of "reasonable expectations." After all, adventure isn't always safe, and parents have a vested interest in keeping their children safe. Amelia Earhart, it might be noted, was lost at sea while piloting her plane across the Pacific.

Spirited Children Are More Powerful

Kyle (age three) yelled at the top of his lungs for an hour and a half in protest against his father's demand that he take a bath. You just don't find that kind of rebellion—much less strength—in your average three-year-old.

When Lisa was fourteen, she and a friend defied her parents' orders and snuck the car out one icy evening to go joyriding. They returned with a crack in the windshield and a bump the size of an egg on the friend's forehead. Power, as we'll see in chapter 4, isn't always upfront and active. Sometimes it's downright sneaky.

John (age seventeen) still lights up a room when he enters it. His big-hearted laughter is contagious, and when he sings in the shower, it is at the top of his lungs. His dad describes him as "a full-out kind of kid—someone who never holds back. He's great now, but, boy, did we go through some awful times trying to teach him to take no for an answer."

Spirited kids seem to have more energy and power than most kids. They do not like to be controlled, and they use their power to thwart attempts to rein in their freedom. It is as if they view the universe as their personal playground on which they should be able to romp, play, and explore unobstructed by the rules and order that limit others. Again, it is not that they are being intentionally bad or "acting out" negative emotions through misbehavior; they simply want what they want and aren't inclined to let much stand in their way of getting it. When channeled effectively, such power is the stuff that creates leadership. Where would Winston Churchill and Franklin Roosevelt have been without the personal power to stand up to Adolf Hitler? At its worst, power is also a calling card of warlords, bullies, and dictators. There again is Adolf Hitler.

Since part of our job as parents sometimes *is* to get in our kids' way by setting limits on behavior, teaching them the rules of the land, and otherwise saying no a lot, it is no small wonder that parents of spirited children wind up in so many power struggles. Understanding these power struggles—and how to deal with them effectively—is the subject of chapter 5.

Spirited Children Are More Persistent

Mother told Donella (age six) that she would make pizza for dinner. But when she went to get the pizza out of the freezer, she was surprised to find that there was none left. She explained to Donella that they would have to have something else, an explanation that did not go over very well. To say the least. Donella cried, "But you promised!" so long and so loudly that her mother finally gave in and ordered a pizza. When it finally arrived, Donella cried and cried, "This is the wrong kind!" because it wasn't exactly like their usual frozen brand.

David (age ten) would play an interactive video game with online players for hour after hour. When his father told him that he needed to do something else, David argued and argued for more time. He just would not take no for an answer.

Megan (age four) hated change. After returning home late one night from a trip, her mother suggested that she needed to take her bath and go straight to bed. But Megan complained, "You always read me a story!" Her mother recognized the signs of an impending tantrum, and decided to go ahead and read her the customary story.

To the average reader, these kids may sound spoiled, but spoiling is a different sort of thing. Spoiling comes from the outside in. In other words, the parent spoils the child by giving him too many privileges, too much freedom, or too many objects. The child learns to expect these things whenever he wants them. When he doesn't get what he wants, he becomes frustrated and complains. Sometimes the complaint becomes a whine, a yell, or a full-fledged tantrum. The child has become spoiled by his parents.

Spirited kids are different in that they are not spoiled into becoming easily frustrated; they are born that way. They seem to have a high capacity to focus on a goal and not give up until they achieve it. When a parent blocks that goal, as in the above example, they become frustrated and emotional but do not give up on the goal. This frustrates the parent, and pretty soon there are two emotionally charged individuals in a struggle for power. The positive side of this equation is that when spirited kids focus on a useful task, their persistence compares favorably to Michelangelo's while painting the Sistine Chapel. When they refuse to be stymied in their pursuit of a goal, they are exemplifying a trait that Alexander Graham Bell needed to invent the telephone, and Bill Gates needed to found Microsoft. This persistence can be a great asset. Most entrepreneurs will tell you that the number-one ingredient in their success was the ability to keep going when others would have quit—to refuse to take no for an answer. This persistence can pay major dividends later on—although it can drive a parent crazy in the short run.

Spirited Children Are More Sensitive

Lauren (age four) complained that her shirt scratched her. When her father checked and didn't see anything wrong, and told her so, Lauren burst into tears, pulled off the shirt, and cried until she fell asleep.

Michael (age ten) was a very gifted and competitive athlete. He didn't just *not like* losing, he hated it. When he was losing, he would yell at his teammates, often abusively, to play better. And when he lost, he would often leave the field or court in tears.

Ben's (age six) mother was sure that her son had ESP, because he had an uncanny ability to read her moods. "He would just know how I felt about something without even asking," she said.

Spirited children are often described as thin skinned, high strung, intuitive, and just plain sensitive. Sometimes this means that, like Lauren, they are physically sensitive to textures, noises, bright lights, and other environmental stimuli that do not bother other children or adults. Other times this means that they are emotionally sensitive to criticism, to slights, and, like Michael, to losing or failing. They can become easily frustrated and fall into tantrums when things do not work out for them. On the positive side, they are often highly attuned not only to their own sensitivities but to those of others. Like Ben, they often have a heightened ability to read other people.

This is not a definitive list of traits that are common to *all* spirited children. You will not find that all spirited children exhibit each of these traits, and you may find other traits that are typical of many other such children. My purpose is to give you an overview of what to look for, not to give you a checklist for making a diagnosis. You will also find that spirited kids vary in the degree to which they exhibit these traits. Some may show their persistence by crying until they fall asleep, while others might be more prone to argue until you wish that they *would* fall asleep.

I also hope that I have made convincingly the point that the traits of a spirited child are a double-edged sword. They have their obvious downside in the conflicts they cause at home, at school, and in the community. But they each have a wonderful upside that, if channeled properly, has great value. Once tamed, the positive aspects of these same traits can lead the child to huge personal successes, as well as to making a significant contribution for the rest of us. Ernest Hemingway, Helen Keller, Ted Turner, and countless other successful men and women—my guess is that all were spirited children who were at least partially tamed by loving parents, teachers, and others and who grew up to use their myriad talents to achieve a success unknown to most of their more conventional peers. If you are the parent of a spirited child, or of a child who shows some of the traits of spirited children, you have an opportunity to help nurture this potential. And who knows? You may have a champion chomping at the bit for his invitation to run in the Kentucky Derby.

The Spirit of the Child

"... most men never reach faith at all. They live a long time in immediacy or spontaneity, finally they advance in some reflection, and then they die ... Most people drift on in such a way that they never become spirit, all their many years of immediacy tend towards spiritual retardation and therefore they never become spent. But the unhappy childhood and youth of the exceptions are transfigured into spirit."

—Soren Kierkegaard
(1813–1855), *Soren Kierkegaard's Journals and Papers*
(1967)

MARK WAS ROUGHHOUSING with his four-year-old son, Chad, on the big chair in the den one day. Roughhousing is a great way to connect with children. It's especially good for fathers, who are sometimes better with actions than with words. The action in roughhousing says, "I like spending time with you; you are important to me; you are fun to play with; I like you." Roughhousing also creates a good opportunity to teach children how to play actively without hurting other children. This lesson, although vital, is often a painful one to learn, especially with spirited kids.

Chad was sitting in Mark's lap while he held his arms and tickled him. Like his older sister, Megan, Chad loved to be tickled. The difference is that Chad is a spirited child, while Megan is not. Mark did not know about spirited children, but he was a keen enough observer of child behavior to recognize a problem before it happened. While holding his son's arms, he noticed that Chad was beginning to throw his head back—in the direction of Mark's nose. So he gave him a warning: "Chad, don't hit me with your head." Chad's response was to arch his back with the force of a striking rattlesnake and snap his head back hard into his father's nose. Mark became enraged as he jumped out of his chair, grasping his nose in acute pain. This action, which of course landed Chad on the floor, was followed by Mark's yelling at him, "Chad! I just told you *not* to hit me with your head!" Chad was dumbstruck by the outburst, because to him, he'd done exactly what his father had told him to do. Hadn't Mark just told him to hit him with his head? Well, not exactly, but to spirited children, the word *don't!* often has no meaning, and so they just hear around it. Mark would have been much better served by saying nothing and making sure that his son's head could not reach his nose by shielding it with one of his hands.

Mark now has a scar on his nose to confirm the wisdom of this lesson. And if you have never been as angry at your child as Mark was at Chad, then I doubt that you have a spirited child. Because having a spirited child means that you experience levels of anger that you never realized you were capable of achieving. You may very well have a scar or two on your body to prove my point.

Your Unique Spirit

Have you ever wondered what it is that makes you uniquely you? Is it your personality? Your looks? The sum total of your achievements? How about your values, attitudes, and beliefs? Maybe it's your behavior or the way you react emotionally to events in your life. Could it be your dreams? Maybe it's the way you decorate your living space. The comedian Steven Wright once joked that thieves had broken into his home and stolen all his belongings—and replaced everything with exact replicas! We are each so unique that it is unlikely that exact replicas of our furnishings, let alone all of the more profound aspects of who we are, exist anywhere in the world.

It's very clear that when you were made, God broke the mold, which is a nice way of saying that God didn't want another person like you—at least not exactly like you. Put another way, that's why nature requires a male and a female to make a baby. If we could reproduce ourselves asexually, like an amoeba, there would be no change to the gene pool. Our children would be exact replicas of us. This would not give the human race the diversity necessary to advance the species, and it would make romantic getaways a lot less interesting.

But what is it that makes you and your child unique persons? What is special at our core that is one of a kind? Even identical twins, who are genetically the same and who share many of the same tastes, behaviors, and countless other similarities, are not exactly the same. Raise them in two different families and compare them years later, and you will find amazing similarities. But look closely, and you will also find significant differences. Can all the differences be accounted for by environment? Perhaps. But there is also the possibility that there exists something additional, something commonly called *spirit*. The word is not new. It pops up in everything from movie trailers to religious sermons, from high school pep rallies to plays about Christmas. How about some of these:

- A triumph of the human spirit
- School spirit
- Free spirit
- The Spirit of St. Louis
- The spirit of Christmas past

- The Great Spirit
- Spirit in the sky
- The American spirit
- *Esprit de corps*
- Keeping your spirits up
- Spirit of the people
- Spirit of the West
- Holy Spirit
- Spirit of the age
- Divine spirit
- Spirituality
- Kindred spirits
- Ghost spirits
- Spirit in a bottle (genie)
- Spirits in a bottle (alcohol)
- That Blue Star spirit (my summer camp)
- High spirits
- Low spirits
- Spirit of adventure
- The spirit of God

The word *spirit* itself seems to connote something a little mysterious that goes beyond the scientifically observable and into the realm of faith and the unknown, down deep to the depths of what makes us who we are. Whether it is viewed as a life force, essence, connection to God, or other primary factor in our lives, there is something at our core that transcends everything else we may think, feel, or do. It is our spirit, and it is uniquely us.

Your child's spirit is a precious thing. It is a gift from some power much greater than you. Though you may not always understand, or even want, the spirit that was given to your child, learning to accept it and value it for what it is can be a powerful step in helping your child succeed and you feel successful. Some spirits are quiet and reflective, while others are downright aggressive. Some seek companionship in their fellow humans, while others prefer solitude. Some seem to be combinations of many qualities. Some are quite spirited.

The Spirited Spirit

Jeffrey's mother came to me at her wit's end. Her red-haired son was, as she called him, "hell on Big Wheels." Everything about him was over the top. From the fact that he was always first up in the morning to the way he rode his Big Wheel tricycle around the cul-de-sac with disregard for life or limb (his own or others), her son had energy and enthusiasm to burn. He wasn't a mean kid. It was just that once his motor got going, his mind seemed to disengage, and normal caution lights got ignored. This got him into trouble at preschool and made him none too popular with the neighbors.

After interviewing Jeffrey and his parents separately, I could see that they were highly discouraged about their child's prospects. They seemed to feel that he had been dealt a bad hand by the gods of genetics and was destined for a life of bouncing off one wall after another (both literally as well as figuratively.) I decided that before we did anything to change Jeffrey's unproductive behavior, they needed a reality check. So I told them, "Your son has a strong spirit."

"Tell me about it," his father responded sarcastically.

"I'm serious," I continued. "Do you have any idea how many kids will grow up to languish passively in the midst of all this opportunity we have in the world today, because they don't have the fire in the belly to go for it? Sure, Jeffrey is a handful now, but he's got that fire that will propel him through life. It's our job to help him handle it sanely."

"You're telling us this is a good thing?" his father asked suspiciously. "Because if this is good, I sure would hate to have a *problem* child."

"Do you know what I think a real problem child is?" I asked him.

"Lizzie Borden?—the one in the old rhyme who axed her parents to death?" came his deadpan reply.

"Well, sure, kids who have serious psychological problems or who are sociopaths, but that's not what I'm talking about right now. I think the real problem children often turn out to be the ones who are overly polite, well mannered, and always intent on doing the right thing so they will be approved by adults. These kids either never had a strong spirit to begin with, or they gave it away in an attempt to be perfect. They look fine on the outside, but eventually they either explode or live lives of quiet desperation," I said, throwing in a little Henry David Thoreau, in case he was the literary type. "Now tell me," I added, sensing that he was hearing me. "Which of the two of you was a spirited child?"

They looked at each other and laughed. "I think we both had a little of that free spirit in us," said Jeffrey's mother. "But neither of us got into a lot of trouble—at least nothing like Jeffrey."

"Spirited children aren't all alike," I reminded them. "Some are more energized than others. Some learn to channel their spirit appropriately, while others need some help in learning to use their gifts within reasonable limits. But I'll tell you this: It is much easier to find ways to get a spirited child to manage his enormous energy effectively than it is to breathe life into a passive child. Your son is a lot of trouble now, but that same spirit that causes so much anguish today is the stuff of champions."

"Right," said his father. "I'll notify the people at Wheaties to get his box ready."

"Let's try this another way," I said. "Each of us has a unique spirit at our core—an essence that makes us who we are. Although no two are exactly alike, there are some similarities. Spirited children tend to be more curious, adventurous, powerful, persistent, and sensitive. Does that sound like anyone you know?"

"Yes, that's pretty much Jeffrey," said the mother. "And that's what's driving us and his teachers crazy!"

"That's because Jeffrey hasn't learned to use these characteristics positively yet," I said. "But can you think of any successful people who were also curious, adventurous, powerful, persistent, and sensitive? Think explorers, inventors, athletes, entrepreneurs, leaders, and others who took these same qualities and turned them into successes."

"Hmm," said his father. "I see where you are going with this. If we can somehow get Jeffrey to use his superpowers for good instead of evil, then we'll have a superhero on our hands."

"Well, maybe not a superhero or even a superstar, but a successful human being isn't hard to imagine," I replied.

"I think we'd both be happy with that," said his mother.

Jeffrey's father looked serious for a moment and then said, "Yes, we'd both be happy with that."

Parenting for the Upside

Most parents of spirited children know the downside of this slippery slope: the tantrums, power struggles, refusals, disrespect, sidetracks, homework battles, and head butts, to name but a few of the challenges likely to be encountered. But like Jeffrey's parents, they usually miss seeing the upside potential also inherent in the spirited spirits of their children.

The Danish philosopher Kierkegaard wrote that childhood is a time of immediacy and spontaneity. You might say that spirited kids exemplify this in spades. They seem to prefer to act first and ask questions later, then move on to the next adventure without considering the consequences of their last actions. While spontaneity can certainly bring about a lot of joy, it can cause them and others a lot of trouble. One of our challenges as parents is to help such children learn to temper the immediacy and spontaneity with an ability to reflect on life, including themselves and others, in a way that sets the stage for a more spiritual and successful life later on. Through taming, we not only bring out the positive aspects of the spirited temperament in a highly pragmatic way, we also begin moving our child to become ready to one day reach those higher levels of being that come with self-reflection and spiritual exploration.

Take a look at the following list of spirited characteristics and how they can play out on either the downside (the wild side) or the upside (the tamed side). Notice also that I have included comments about how the child moves psychologically within each of these traits. Observing behavior from a movement point of view gives a deeper understanding of the child's inner world, or as the saying goes, "If you want to understand what a person really thinks, don't listen to the tongue in his mouth, but watch the tongue in his shoe." While you are reading this list, think about your own child and bear in mind that where he turns out on this chart depends a lot on the parenting he receives along the way.

Characteristic	DOWNSIDE (WILD)	UPSIDE (TAMED)
CURIOUS	• Being easily distracted makes it difficult for him to finish tasks	• Highly interested in knowledge of all kinds
		• well informed
	• disregards rules and the rights of others to satisfy his need to know	• eager to learn
		• tempers his natural curiosity with the rights of others

Characteristic	DOWNSIDE (WILD)	UPSIDE (TAMED)
CURIOUS (*cont.*)	• coupled with his adventurous trait, will often find trouble and persue it • moves where angels fear to tread.	• capable of coming up with new ideas and approaches • may develop an interest in spiritual matters, psychology, or philosophy in order to find answers • moves boldly (yet reasonably) where he has not gone before.
ADVENTUROUS	• Ignores rules and rights of others • often out of control • dangerous thrill-seeking behavior can include frequent accidents, drugs, sex, violence • moves haphazardly.	• Takes courageous, reasonable risks • develops talents • participates in sports, clubs, and other positive activities • likes to learn, explore, try new things • moves forward.
POWERFUL	• Likes to boss others around or show them that they can't boss him • may become tyrannical • prone to tantrums and explosive outbursts • moves to overcome others.	• Learns how to get what he wants without hurting or alienating others • strong leader • able to withstand peer pressure • makes things happen • moves to overcome obstacles.
PERSISTENT	• Nags, whines, annoys, and otherwise drives you crazy to get what he wants • will continue chasing the cheese down the wrong path regardless of negative results or punishment	• Argues intelligently and respectfully for what he wants • is able to withstand hardship and disappointment in pursuit of a goal

Characteristic	DOWNSIDE (WILD)	UPSIDE (TAMED)
PERSISTENT (*cont.*)	• doesn't know when to give up and is slow to learn from mistakes • easily addicted • moves in mindless repetition.	• able to focus and stay on task for long periods of time • learns when to give up and when to keep trying • recognizes his addictive nature and avoids likely temptations • moves steadily in the direction of his goals.
SENSITIVE	• Easily bothered and annoyed • constantly complains about things not being right • wants the world to revolve around her needs • believes that others are unfair, critical, or harsh • moves away from others.	• Highly aware and attuned to pain and suffering, whether his own or that of others • concerned about the needs of others, the community, even the planet • understands self and takes action to handle her own needs without trampling on others • moves to help others.

The upside holds great promise for spirited children. When tamed by a loving parent and/or other concerned adults, such children learn to use their incredible gifts for the benefit of themselves and others. This is why we do not seek to break their spirits, their wills, or anything else about these spirited children. We do not want to extinguish the fire or change their basic natures. What we want is to redirect them away from the downside risks of their spirits to their upside potential. The methods presented in the remainder of this book will give you skills for doing just that.

Taming Versus Breaking

"... but a boy's will is his life, and he dies when it is broken, as the colt dies in harness, taking a new nature in becoming tame. Rarely has the boy felt kindly towards his tamers. Between him and his master has always been war."

—HENRY ADAMS (1838–1918),
American historian, journalist,
and novelist, *The Education of
Henry Adams*

"I once heard a judicious father say, 'He would treat his child as he would his horse: First convince it that he was its master, and then its friend.'"

—MARY WOLLSTONECRAFT
(1759–1797), *Thoughts on the
Education of Daughters*

THE TWO QUOTES that I've chosen for the introduction to this chapter may confuse you. They suggest that taming and breaking are the same thing and that both are necessary aspects of effective parenting. In this chapter, I want to distinguish between these two terms and explain why *taming* a child's spirit can be accomplished without *breaking* the child's will. This difference notwithstanding, there is wisdom in these two quotes as well.

To Break or Not to Break

For over twenty years, I've been teaching parents through our video-based *Active Parenting* programs that the purpose of parenting is to "protect and prepare children to survive and thrive in the kind of society in which they will live." This idea of parenting within a historical context means that how our cave-dwelling ancestors needed to parent differed from our biblical ancestors, which differed from parents in Henry Adams's and Mary Wollstonecraft's times, which differs from our own. As society has moved from more autocratic leadership models (survival of the fittest; that is, the guy with the biggest club) to kings, queens and peasants, to the rule of law, to our modern democratic trends (and remember, modern democracy is less than 250 years old—a blink of the eye in evolutionary terms)—the role of parents has also needed to change and keep pace.

For example, for much of human history, parents have treated their children as favored slaves. To be sure, they were often kind and loving, but the bottom line was that children were to obey their parents at all costs. A disobedient child in biblical days could actually be taken to the gates of the city and stoned to death. This made sense in a world where everyone knew his place and talking back to those in superior positions could lead to death for adults. In order to survive in such a society, children needed to learn blind obedience and make it a habit. A spirited child who exercised his will against his parents had to be broken for his own sake as well as for the perceived sake of the community. After all, the conventional wisdom was that too much power in the hands of the wrong class could lead to rebellion. So society essentially told parents, "Either break your child's will to resist, or we'll just kill him when he grows up." And a lot of spirited kids were broken so that they became docile members of their society (and survived, but never thrived). And a lot of others grew up to be killed by society (trying to thrive, but failing to survive). Since survival is a higher priority than thriving for most parents, they usually opted for our autocratic parenting traditions that beat children down with harsh punishments until their wills were broken and they accepted their own form of slavery. Children were "seen and not heard," "spoke only when spoken to," and always seemed to be saddled with the job of taking out the garbage.

However, society evolved. Kings lost their absolute power, slavery ended, and democracy reared its egalitarian head. The king-servant/master-slave relationship that existed between parents and children for much of history became outdated as soon as slavery and monarchy disappeared from society as a whole. Of course, this doesn't mean that many parents don't still treat their children as property, just that such parenting now often leads to rebellion rather than submission.

And here's the first problem with attempting to break a spirited child: it's a lot harder to do than it once was. After two hundred years of responding to tyranny with rebellion, children seem to almost intuitively grasp the unfairness of heavy-handed discipline methods. It makes them angry and motivates them to resist harder. Spirited children, who are already into power and persistence, will hold out for hours when they perceive that they are being treated unfairly. Their tantrums can make the Boston Tea Party look like, well, a tea party.

The second problem with breaking a child's will is that she may very well need that will later in life. People who know their place, speak only when spoken to, and otherwise take a docile, subservient position in society may survive, but they rarely thrive in our competitive, free-market world. If you want your child to go for the gusto, be all that she can be, and otherwise take advantage of the wonderful opportunities offered in a free society, she is going to benefit from having that strong unbroken will. Add to that the need to resist peer pressure—not just during adolescence, but throughout one's life—and breaking your child's will is a lot like breaking your pet bird's wing and then setting her free.

Finally, a third problem with breaking children is found in the opening quote by Henry Adams: "Rarely has the boy felt kindly towards his tamers. Between him and his master has always been war." Remember, when Adams uses the word *tamers,* he is using it as a synonym for *breakers.* Back in Adams's time, this was accomplished with harsh discipline and frequent visits to the woodshed. And just as a horse tamer would beat a horse into submission, a parent was expected to beat his child into submission. The price for such tactics, as pointed out by Adams, is in the damage it does to the relationship ("between him and his master has always been war"). Perhaps the relationship didn't matter that much if all you wanted the horse to do was wear blinders and pull your carriage. But suppose you were the Lone Ranger and depended on your horse Silver to save your masked face from certain disaster every episode; I think you might want him to feel at peace with you rather than at war. ("Silver, I've been shot in the leg, go get help before I bleed to death." "Sure, boss, and by the way, did I ever thank you for all those beatings? Oh, and if I'm not back in thirty days, feel free to go ahead and die.")

The relationship we have with our children is not just important because it's what makes parenting a joy. It's important because it's the relationship that gives you the power to influence your child the most. When you have a good relationship with your child, she is likely to pay attention and even follow your guidance when you say, "Honey, tobacco is a dangerous, dangerous drug that not only makes your skin yellow, your breath stink, and your face age before its time, it can also kill you slowly and painfully. I love you and want you to grow up strong and healthy. So don't even try one of those stinking things." However, when you are at war with your child, and your relationship is filled with resentment, if you say anything at all on the matter of smoking, it will probably be along the lines of, "If I catch you smoking, you are grounded for life. Do you understand?" Sure your child understands, as she thinks, "I'll be damned if I'll let that %#$& run my life anymore. I'll smoke if I want to. I just won't get caught!"

Without a positive relationship, a parent's influence is often the reverse of what the parent intends. In other words, your child understands what you want and strives to even the score by doing the opposite. He becomes a "reverse puppet." You pull the string to make the right arm go up, and he raises the left arm. You give a yank on the string that controls the right leg, and, lo and behold, the left leg comes up (and often kicks you in the shin!). This sort of revenge for perceived injustices is all too common a motivation for kids who have had their spirits trampled by overbearing parents. So strong is the desire to defeat such parents that the teen would actually be willing to sacrifice himself in the process. In fact, I have told more than one teenager while working with him in therapy that it takes a lot of courage to do what is really in your own best interest when it is also something that your parents want you to do.

This book is not about breaking our children. It's about taming them in ways that build a loving relationship and set the foundation for them to survive and thrive in the kind of society in which they will live. It is about teaching kids to accept authority gracefully and to learn how to interact effectively with it rather than bristle and buck against it. It is about teaching them to become responsible, respectful, cooperative, courageous human beings who can give and take in concert with other human beings. Old-school methods of breaking a child's will do not accomplish these goals.

What are these outdated methods of discipline that continue to hang on despite their failure to work? There is not an exhaustive list, but the following will give you an idea:

- Establishing the superiority of the parent over the child.
- Making sure that the child fears the parent.
- Relying on punishments, often severe, physical, and humiliating.
- Using rewards as bribes for following orders.
- Overusing time-outs and grounding.
- Applying anger, yelling, and other intimidation techniques while refusing to tolerate the same by the child.
- Withholding affection and love for misbehavior, lack of effort, and even perceived underachievement.
- Emphasizing blind obedience rather than problem solving.

If these methods sound familiar, it's because most of us experienced some or all of them while growing up and have used some or all of them with our own children. This is the basic autocratic old-school model of parenting that has been around for centuries. In today's modern, democratic world, as I have said, it often leads to resistance and rebellion, making matters worse rather than better. When it does work to break the child, the results are often sad: a broken child who has neither the God-given will nor spirit to succeed in today's complex world.

Hold the Reins Loosely (but Hold the Reins)

First, let me make one point absolutely clear: while I have little use for the autocratic approach to parenting spirited children, I have even less use for the newer permissive styles. Parents who make the mistake of allowing the downside qualities of spirited children free reign make a terrible mistake. When parents fail to address problems, set limits, and otherwise take the leadership role in the family, these kids do not just magically "grow out of it." They usually get worse, ending up in trouble at school and in the community. Untamed, their natural gifts are buried under the weight of excess. Instead of Buffalo Bill, they become Billy the Kid, their spirited temperaments out of control and dangerous. So please understand that I am not advocating letting spirited kids "get away with it." Nor do I believe that if you just love them enough all will work out in the end. Spirited kids need to be taught how to use their CAPPS (curiosity, adventurousness, power, persistence, and sensitivity) within reasonable limits for the good of themselves and others. Like beautiful, wild horses, they need either to live in the wild, or they need to be tamed (not broken). And they are not likely to tame themselves.

The difference between taming and breaking is partially about goals. The goal of breaking is to make the child into an obedient, even docile, conformist who will not cause adults trouble and will be easily led by authority into whatever direction thought advisable. The Fascists of the 1930s and 1940s in Germany were able to come to power, in part, because an authoritarian culture had already broken the spirit of the people and made them easy to lead. The goal of taming, on the other hand, is to help spirited children live in harmony with others while building on the upside of their unique qualities. Their differences are respected, even admired, and while they are brought back into the herd, they are still able to maintain their individuality and free will.

The other difference between taming and breaking—and the difference that is pertinent to the rest of this book—has to do with parenting methods. In contrast to the authoritarian methods of the child breakers and the permissive inaction of those who indulge children, taming requires a combination of firm leadership and relationship building. If this sounds reminiscent of Mary Wollstonecraft's quote about being both master and friend to a child, it is. However, it's important to remember that leaders are no longer masters, and that although there are many similarities between tamers and friends, parenting requires some things that friendship does not. The following eight-point model for taming a spirited child will give you an overview of where we are going in this book and help establish a mental picture before we tackle the specifics.

An Eight-Sided Taming Corral

Imagine a corral, much like the corrals used to tame wild horses, but with eight distinct sides. Each plank of this octagon represents a set of ideas and skills needed to tame your spirited child. None of them, as you will have guessed by now, includes a whip or a bit. As you and your child interact inside this corral, she will from time to time bolt toward one or another of the eight sides, requiring you to respond with the skills, support, or other information contained there.

Because these eight sides work together in concert, I urge you to read the entire book before using *any* of these strategies. Otherwise, you may find your child bolting through a hole in the ring that you did not know existed. For example, you may be working on the relationship-building side of the octagon when your child suddenly requires discipline. If you respond with your old discipline methods, not yet having read the chapters on discipline, you may undermine your relationship-building efforts. Moreover, you might have found something in the prevention section that could have enabled you to anticipate and avoid the problem altogether.

I realize it is a challenge to keep eight separate areas in mind at once. To help refresh your memory at the end of the book, I have added a chapter 14 entitled "Your Taming Plan in Action." This chapter is both a review of the skills and information we will be covering and an action plan for applying them in your own family. As you read through the eight planks of the taming corral, you will notice that I have added chapter numbers to the side. These indicate the chapters in which these concepts and skills are primarily found. However, they are not limited to those chapters; neither are those chapters limited to those concepts. The purpose of these planks is to prepare you for what is coming and to help you structure your mind to remember these eight areas.

Plank 1. Leadership (chapters 1–4)

Establish yourself as a firm yet friendly leader in the family. Show respect to your children and expect them to show respect in return. Use a firm and friendly tone of voice; allow input and freedom within limits. Be confident, while recognizing that all parents make mistakes—and so will you.

Plank 2. Prevention (chapters 1, 2, and 10)

Anticipate and prevent problems. Understand your child's unique CAPPS (curiosity, adventurousness, power, persistence, and sensitivity). Learn what triggers CAPPS and how to defuse them beforehand. Learn to redirect your child to use these traits in positive ways. Understand the dynamics of anger and how to handle this primary emotion.

Plank 3. Relationship (chapters 4 and 9)

Establish a positive relationship with your child, building on the friendship aspects of parenting. Make time and develop the skills to establish ties with your child. Provide sincere and realistic encouragement on a regular basis.

Plank 4. Power (chapter 5)

Understand the principles of power and learn to sidestep power struggles. Your spirited child can sometimes seem "power drunk," so learn how to teach him to manage this powerful quality and use it for motivation and not intimidation. Learn the same lessons for yourself if need be.

Plank 5. Structure (chapter 6)

Provide structure for your child to help her learn to live within limits. These structures operate like corrals helping a wild horse learn to accept limits to his freedom as the handler works to tame him. Understand that spirited children need a flexible structure. Like buildings constructed in an earthquake-prone environment, a rigid structure will crack and break under the stress. Modern earthquake-proof buildings use a flexible structure that is able to withstand the impact. Learn to focus your use of structure on time, space, and behavior.

Plank 6. Discipline (chapters 7, 8, and 9)

Use respectful forms of discipline to enforce the limits of the situation. Avoid discipline that is too harsh, but do not fail to offer discipline as needed. Understand the interaction between discipline, empathy, and problem solving, and use that understanding to teach your child to live within the limits while getting her needs met at the same time.

Plank 7. Problems (chapter 11)

Teach your child to problem solve. Help him identify alternative solutions and anticipate consequences. Teach him to identify his feelings as well as his wants. Use effective communication skills to provide opportunities for teaching empathy for others.

Plank 8. Resources (chapter 12)

Recognize the need for help in taming spirited children and identify where in your community that help is available. Reach out to the school, spiritual organizations, recreational leagues, mental health professionals, family and friends, and others as much as possible.

There is a tendency to think that spirited children want to remain unbridled, free, wild even. We think that they will resist all efforts to rein them in whether by taming, breaking or any other means. But the truth is that all children long, at some level, for someone to tame them. Spirited children, although they may put on a show of independence and rebellion, are not at all happy with their state of affairs. They want to know that someone is bigger, smarter, stronger, and more capable than they are—someone who will help them connect and be a part of the fold. It is a relief for them to find this tamer.

The Tamer as Friend

*Nobody sees a flower—really—it is so small it takes time—we
haven't time—and to see takes time, like to have a friend takes
time.*

—Georgia O'Keeffe

(1887–1986), American artist

THERE IS AN old African folktale about a boy who had lost his
mother. When his father remarried, the boy was still grieving his
mother's death and was both cold and rebellious toward his stepmother. She was a good-hearted woman who tried everything she
could think of to get him to mind her, but to no avail. The more she
pushed and prodded, the more defiant he became. Finally, in desperation, the woman went to see a tribal healer. She told him her story and
asked him to make a love potion to give to her son so that they could
have a good relationship. The old man listened to her story and then
told her that he could help, but to do so he would need a whisker from
a furious mountain lion.

The woman was shocked by the task she had been given, but she
loved her husband and wanted to be a good mother to her stepson,
so she set out toward the mountains where the lions lived. Soon she
found lion tracks that led to a cave on the side of a mountain. She
quietly walked up to the mouth of the cave and took from her sack
some raw meat, placing it on the ground. She then walked a hundred
paces away and hid in the bushes. Soon the mountain lion came out

of the cave and smelled the meat. He looked around and then, sensing it was safe, ate his gift. The woman came back the next day with some more meat. Again she left it at the mouth of the cave, but this time only walked fifty feet away and stood in the open. Each day for a week, she came back with meat, and each time she stood a little closer to the feasting lion. Eventually the lion ate from her hand while she gently stroked his fur. Finally, she was able to pull a whisker from his chin while he ate.

She returned to the tribal healer with the whisker and asked him to make good on his promise to make a love potion to heal her rebellious son. But the wise old healer said that he would make no such potion. Instead he told her that she must approach her stepson in the same manner as she did the mountain lion, slowly and patiently. During the days that followed, she did just this, and within ten weeks she and her stepson had become best friends.

The Myth That You Can't Be Your Child's Friend

One of the most popular current sayings about parenting, whether by parents or professionals, is that you can't be your child's friend. This information is almost always said in the negative. Sometimes it's said directly to a parent, as in, "Well, you can't be your child's friend, you know!" Sometimes it's said more globally, as if it holds the key to understanding all the problems parents experience with their children, as in, "Parents are too busy trying to be their child's friend!"

It seems to me that there are two problems with this advice: it is wrong, and it is bad advice. It is wrong because you most definitely *can* be your child's friend. That is if you consider friendship to be based on mutual respect, having fun together, sharing, support, encouragement, spending time together, solving problems together, and generally liking each other. When people say that "you can't be your child's friend," what they really mean is, "Parents have to discipline their children, while friends don't." And in this way, being a parent does differ from being a peer. When I was a camp director training staff to work with children, I said it another way. I told my staff that it was important to play with their campers and have a good time together, but the counselor was the one who played with one eye on the clock. In other words, the one in charge, whether a counselor or a parent, is the one who says it's time to stop and get ready for what comes next. The person in charge is also the one who makes sure that rules aren't broken and that activities stay within reasonable limits of health, safety, and accepted values.

There is certainly a difference between a peer-peer friendship and a parent-child friendship, just as there are differences regarding friendships between persons of the same sex and those between persons of the opposite sex and those between persons of vastly different ages. But these differences do not negate the concept of friendship. They just recognize that in some friendships the two parties involved play different roles. In a parent-child relationship, parents play the role of leader and authority in the family, while children are more often in the learner and participant role. Parents must make decisions regarding health, safety, and family values for themselves as well as for their children, while children make decisions only within the limits that their parents deem appropriate for their age and level of responsibility. And parents must sometimes say no to their children's desires.

This role of no sayer is where some parents get too caught up with wanting to be liked by their child to risk the child's disappointment or wrath. Without the skills to say no effectively (skills we will cover in chapters six through eight), these parents get into a terrible cycle of giving in to more and more unreasonable demands until a spirited child has become a spirited brat. I suspect this is exactly where parents who love to say "you can't be your child's friend" are coming from. But in truth, even friends must learn to say no to friends.

So saying no to your child's unreasonable demands does not exclude your being your child's friend.

Now on to my second problem: Saying you can't be your child's friend is bad advice. Not only *can* you be your child's friend, but it's something to strive for, not avoid. Old-school parenting taught that parents must maintain a superior-inferior relationship with their children. This is hardly the stuff of friendship. And if you were unfortunate enough to have a spirited child, then you'd better make yourself the master and break that inferior's will fast. The problem with such an approach in modern times is that today's children, as I've pointed out in earlier chapters, tend to rebel at such treatment rather than knuckle under. This is especially true of spirited children. On the other hand, taming a spirited child by making friends slowly and patiently, much like the stepmother and the mountain lion (and her stepson) can have the child eating out of your hand before very long.

Winning Your Spirited Child's Friendship

Friendships of any kind often seem to materialize out of nowhere, without any effort from either party. But with a closer look, you will find certain ingredients that most have in common. Although some friendships do evolve easily, others require a good deal of effort and intention on the part of one or both parties. With spirited kids and their parents, there has usually been so much conflict in the relationship that friendship is pretty far from anyone's mind. Years of power struggles, tantrums, anger, and punishment have left both sides feeling frayed, frazzled, and hurt. To build a friendship at this point will take some effort, but it can be done. And because friendship is a joyful experience, the bond that can blossom between a parent and child is one of the most joyful experiences we can know.

But there is another reason that building a friendship with your child is so important. When kids like being with their parents, when they experience joy in the relationship themselves, they are more inclined to want to cooperate rather than rebel. This also gives parents much more influence in the choices their child will make, influence that can be the difference in everything from misbehavior to using drugs.

Winning a positive relationship with your spirited child—becoming friends—takes more than patience and time, it also requires strategy and skill. The African stepmother didn't just run up to the mountain lion's cave and give the lion's whiskers a yank. This would have been a recipe for disaster (as well as a recipe for a tasty stepmother), and the story would have had an unhappy ending for everyone— except perhaps for the mountain lion, who was destined to eat well that day either way. Instead, the courageous and loving mother came up with a strategy based on her knowledge of mountain lions and used that knowledge gradually to win his trust and affection.

F-R-I-E-N-D, the Acronym

To help you develop your own strategy, I've come up with a simple acronym for *friend* that will give you some ideas about how to proceed. This is not a definitive list of what it takes to build a friendship, just some keys that I've seen over and over again between friends of many kinds, especially between parents and children. Your own knowledge of your child will help you tweak this list to suit your own parenting style and the particulars of your child.

> **F**: *Fun*
> **R**: *Respect*
> **I**: *Interests*
> **E**: *Encouragement*
> **N**: *No*
> **D**: *Delight*

F Is for Fun

Ever notice that most friendships involving a young person start out with sharing fun together? As we get older, we can often talk our way into a friendship, but when we are kids or young adults, we tend to become friends with people we have fun with. When we laugh with someone, enjoy an activity together, or have fun in any way, chemicals called endorphins are released in our bloodstream that make us feel good. That sense of feeling good is then associated with the person with whom we shared the fun experience. This is basic Pavlovian conditioning. The subconscious thinking is something along the lines of "I feel good when I'm with you, so I like being with you, so I like you, so let's be friends, so I can have this good feeling more often. (But please stop ringing that bell; it makes me salivate.)" You get the idea. Have fun with your kids, and you've taken a huge step toward taming your child. If this sounds simple, it's not.

The problem most parents of spirited children have is that they don't always *like* their child. This is nothing to be ashamed about. Spirited kids have great potential, but their day-to-day CAPPS (curious, adventurous, powerful, persistent, and sensitive) behavior can often make them a pain to be around. Parents, being human, often stop trying to engage these kids in fun activities, figuring that it is safer to let sleeping dogs (and mountain lions) lie. Although this strategy does bring an opportunity for a little rest and relaxation, it does nothing to improve the relationship. And without a good relationship, you can't get the mountain lion's whiskers. So, the first step in taming your child is actually to begin having fun together. If you are already having fun together, keep it up and look for creative ways to expand that fun.

What are some ways to have fun together? Use your knowledge of your child to help, but consider some of these methods:

- **Board games.** Also good for improving their minds and teaching social skills like fair play, sportsmanship, and taking turns. Be careful of Monopoly, though; it can turn cutthroat on you in an instant!

- **Sports activities.** If you saw the movie *Field of Dreams,* you'll recall that it isn't a good idea to wait until after you have died to play catch with your child.

- **Computer and video games.** This is a good opportunity for your child to teach you something, which has the added benefit of building his self-esteem. But be careful if your child tends to get wound up on violence.

- **Roughhousing.** This is a great way to connect, especially with parents who aren't great verbal communicators. But with spirited kids, again, be careful of winding them up. If your child has a hard time calming down afterward, as many spirited children do, better keep your roughhousing to a minimum. It is a myth that these kids need to burn off energy. Getting their engines burning often just produces more fuel for their systems. Many spirited kids would do better learning how to calm themselves. See chapter 10 for some ideas about how to do so.

- **Hands-on creative play.** Spirited kids love Play-Doh, modeling clay, finger painting, playing with sand, and other tactile enterprises. Keep plenty on hand and make time to join in.

- **Acting.** Many spirited kids are quite imaginative and love to dress up, put on plays and puppet shows, and otherwise entertain. You can participate sometimes and be the audience sometimes. And if you are a little bolder, get out the video camera and make a movie together. Then later you can have some quiet time watching it together. I have some great home videos of Ben putting on puppet shows and one especially engaging "Hans and Franz" impression in which my wife caught our six-year-old son attempting to "pump you up!"

- **Watching TV, movies, or home videos together.** Yes, I know, most kids do spend far too much time watching instead of doing. However, there is still a place for some old-fashioned couch-potato entertainment-driven viewing time together. The key is to find something you both enjoy and watch it together. Even better, with younger children, get them on your lap for some snuggle time while you watch. But don't overdo it. We had a no-TV rule in our home for school nights, but relaxed it on weekends. Then later, as the kids got older and were handling school well, we let them watch one or two favorite shows during the week. In fact, these became very happy family times when we all gathered in the den like the Simpsons and let Hollywood entertain us as a family.

- **Reading together or to them.** Reading to your child is not only fun, it's the best thing you can do to improve his or her academic performance. Start while kids are young and continue until they start locking you out of their rooms during adolescence. And when they are old enough to read, take turns or try reading poems or plays together. Spirited children often find being read to a very calming activity that helps defuse a building activity level. When you find your young child starting to lose it, try pulling out a favorite book and curling up in a big chair together.

- **Laughing together.** There is nothing like shared laughter to build a bond of friendship between two people. Watching comedies or reading humorous books together are easy ways to get the endorphins flowing. But you can also learn to use your own sense of humor to add fun to any situation. And you can encourage your child to use his. Of course, you'll want to teach him to avoid disrespectful humor and humor that hurts. But a little self-effacing humor or friendly lampooning can go a long way. Sometimes a parent or other adult can even use humor to defuse an upset spirited child. For example, a teacher once told me about a kindergarten student who was homesick. The child went up to his teacher, a six-foot four-inch man and cried, "I miss my mommy!" The teacher looked down from his high vantage point at the little fellow and then broke into crocodile tears, crying, "I miss my mommy too!" The little boy's tears turned to laughter at the site of this giant crying for his mommy!

- **Water play.** I'm not sure why, although I suspect it has something to do with sensory processing, but playing in or with water seems to have a calming effect on many spirited kids. Bath time with young kids is a great time to play. Add some music and tub toys, and you can have a ball together. You can also let your child play in the sink, or even set up a special basin with water, toys, and other safe objects to play with. In summer, a trip to the swimming pool, lake, or ocean can be a great locale for fun together.

A few helpful hints:

- **Every day a little play.** If you spend most of the day with your child, you shouldn't have trouble finding time to have fun together. But if you work outside the home as well as inside of it, then you will have to be more focused on making time. The key is to have some fun together every day. It can be as brief as ten minutes on weekdays, longer on weekends, but do it every day, and you will see your relationship blossom.

- **Find things you both enjoy doing.** Having fun together means that *both* of you are having fun. If you martyr yourself doing things you hate, you aren't likely to be much fun to play with. Find things that you both enjoy and have fun together so that you can enjoy each other. And if you are one of those stiff-necked adults who don't really know how to have fun, it's time to learn. Let your child teach you. Or as we used to say in the twentieth century, "Get in touch with your inner child."

- **Learn to set limits.** Remember what I said about the camp counselor being the friend who plays with one eye on the clock? It's up to you as the parent to make sure that the fun you share is safe, healthy, and within the values of your family. To do this effectively, you will need to be able to exercise appropriate discipline from time to time. If you are playing a board game together, and your child continues to steal money from the bank to buy hotels (I told you Monopoly could get ugly), you need to set some limits without getting upset yourself. Chapters 6 through 8 will give you some ideas about how to do this with spirited kids.

- **Watch out for what you wind up.** Because spirited kids are more active and powerful than others, once they are going full throttle, they tend to keep going hard. These kids live full out, which can be a very good thing in the right situation. But twenty minutes before dinner, homework, or bedtime is not a good time to get them revved up. Find quieter, fun activities for these times and other times when you know you will want them calm in the near future, and save the high-energy play for the playground, backyard, ball field, or when there is plenty of winding-down time to follow.

R Is for Respect

Friendship may begin with having fun together, but if it does not include mutual respect between the two friends, it quickly turns to yet another casual acquaintance or, worse yet, enmity. Virtually all people raised in democratic societies expect to be treated with respect, whether from the cashier at the grocery store, the police officer writing a speeding ticket, a boss, an employee, a friend, or a spouse. We expect it from our children, and—this may come as a surprise—they expect it from us as well. Respect is so much a part of the fabric of democratic life that to be treated disrespectfully creates an unacceptable tear in the relationship that requires serious repair.

Old-school parenting taught that respect was a one-way street owned by the parents. Our children were expected to treat us respectfully, while we were entitled to treat them any way we wanted short of abuse—and even that line sometimes got a little fuzzy. Since most parents still disrespect their children at one time or another, check the following list to see where you may have slipped. Then resolve to catch yourself in the future before you slip and to find respectful ways to communicate. Some of these examples will seem obvious to you. Others are more subtle. And if you have doubt about any of these items, here's your acid test: Imagine an adult friend doing any of these to *you* and think about how you would feel.

Examples of Ways Parents Disrespect Their Children
- We yell at them. ("How many times do I have to tell you to clean up your room?!")
- We curse at them. ("You think you're so smart, you little bastard!")
- We attack their personality. ("You're so lazy!")
- We refuse to let them defend themselves or argue their point of view. ("I don't want to hear it!")

- We ignore them until they whine to be heard, and then we attack them for whining. ("Stop that awful whining!")
- We always have to have our own way. ("My home, my rules.")
- We don't introduce them to other adults when they are standing right there.
- We pull rank instead of giving a sound reason for our decisions. ("Because I'm the parent, and I said so.")
- We withdraw love, spank them, put them down, or otherwise try to hurt them when they misbehave. ("I have nothing to say to you.")
- We use threats to coerce them. ("If you make another sound, you're going to get it, mister!")
- (Add one or two of your own here . . .)

If one of our friends acted this way toward us, we would probably jettison that friend in a hurry. We all want our children to respect us, but as the author Bernard Malamud once said, "Respect is what you have to have in order to get." Taming our kids also means learning how to treat them respectfully.

Respecting Our Children's Feelings, Wishes, and Beliefs

We want our friends to show us the respect that we feel is due us. But then again, we want everyone else to show us respect. What makes friendship respect different (and better) is that we feel that our friends understand us. They understand our feelings, our wishes, and our beliefs—and they respect them. We feel like they are on our side. They want us to be happy. So, avoiding the negative pitfalls of disrespect is only the first part of respecting our children. The other half is to learn to listen to how they feel, what they want, and how they think, and to respect them for it. No, this doesn't mean giving in to their unreasonable demands or spoiling them. The parent's job is still to set limits, say no sometimes, and provide discipline. How you do this, however, can be for better or for worse. As a foundation for effective discipline, think about how you communicate your respect for your child's feelings, wishes, and beliefs. Do you say things like . . .

- "You are really upset about how scratchy these socks feel, aren't you?"
- "I can hear how much you want to stay home from school today."
- "You think she really has it in for you, don't you?"
- "It's hard having to go to bed when there is so much you want to do, isn't it?"
- "You wish there were no rules about other people's property, so you could just explore anything, right?"
- "You are starting to get wound up."
- "I hear how frustrating that is for you."

Notice that none of these words solves the problem. But they all communicate respect for the child and signal him that you are on his side—that you are his friend. Learning to identify your child's feelings, wishes, and thoughts, and then responding by putting them into words can help defuse sensitive situations and begin to solve problems. In fact, just feeling understood is sometimes enough to change the emotional flavor of a bad situation. We will explore this important area more in chapter 11.

I Is for Interests

Friends share many common interests. Even more important, they show interest in what their friends are interested in even when they don't share that interest. Because they are interested in their friends, they show interest in what their friends are into. You don't have to go skateboarding with your ten-year-old to let him know that you are interested in his favorite activity. You can talk to him about skateboarding, watch a video about it together, ask him what tricks he is learning, and look for opportunities to encourage his interest.

When our son, Ben, was into skateboarding and wanted a half-pipe for our yard, my wife and I helped him research it on the internet. We even went as far as to talk with a carpenter about what it would cost to build one. A half-pipe, if you aren't into skateboarding, is a series of ramps made of wood or concrete that skateboarders use to defy death while thrilling themselves with tricks that put parents into seizures. The more we researched half-pipes, the more we realized that we would be half out of our minds to install one in our yard. Fortunately for us, the carpenter's wife was talking sense to him (legal-liability sense!) at the same time that we were discussing it at home. The fact that we never built the ramp did not diminish the goodwill we earned by being genuinely interested in Ben's favorite hobby. We settled, by the way, on some much safer plastic ramps that we found on another internet site.

I realize that some parents go overboard with their children's interests, but in truth, I find that to be the exception. Parent involvement is usually a positive thing, and although kids sometimes act as if they don't want or need our interest, the message of caring and concern feels good to them on some level. There are a lot of ways to communicate your interest in your child, including the following:

- **Take time to talk.** Busy kids and busy parents often fail to talk about what's going on in their children's lives. Find quiet times when you can tune out the business of the world and really focus on what your child is interested in at the time. Maybe it's during snuggle time before bed, at the kitchen table during a snack, or while driving to one of those many activities kids participate in these days. (You can actually talk about the activity!)

- **Show up at activities.** I'm not one who believes that parents need to be there for every stroke of the baseball bat in their child's life. Kids do need to learn to enjoy activities for the activity's sake and not just to perform for an audience. However, parents who show up some or most of the time send a powerful message that they are interested in their child. This is particularly important for school activities: parent-teacher meetings, parent association programs, performances, and other activities. This let's your child know that you are interested in his school career and want him to succeed. When you are out of town or have another important reason not to be there, a phone call or even flowers (when appropriate) can keep you involved and show that you care.

- **Teach your child skills.** A great way to build the bond with your child is to take time to teach her skills that she shows an interest in. This can be anything from working on a sports skill together, to teaching her a favorite family recipe, to showing her how to change the car's oil. With younger kids, there are a million life skills that you can teach, from tying shoeslaces to cutting up carrots. Just make sure that the skill is age appropriate. In other words, don't try teaching your three-year-old to tie his shoelaces, or you will both wind up frustrated.

- **Encourage your child to teach *you*.** Find out what your child is interested in that you might like to learn yourself. How to make a special mud pie? The latest video game? Nuclear fusion? It doesn't really matter; what matters is that you have a sincere interest to learn and that your child gets to school you! It's great for his self-esteem and even better for the relationship.

- **Learn together.** Find something you are both interested in and then learn about it together. Get a book about it and read together. Search the internet. Take a course. Practice a skill together. Apply what you've learned together. Just don't try to check into the freshman dorm with her when she goes off to college.

A few tips will help you keep your expression of interest on the positive side of the road:

- **Be encouraging.** Use positive language when talking with your child about her interests. Words and phrases like "interesting," "I see," "I didn't know that," "hmm," "nice," "Wow, you really know this stuff!" "fascinating," and "cool" can let her know you are really interested.

- **Be genuine.** Of course, if you are just faking enthusiasm, she will see right through you, and your credibility will be shot. So, if you cannot find some genuine interest in something, it's OK to say, "Hmm, I love how much you are enjoying this. Let me know how it goes."

- **Avoid being critical, judgmental, or otherwise dampening his enthusiasm.** If you always have a tendency to want to make things better, be on guard. If you come across as taking over, being a know-it-all, or always pointing out what can be improved, your child is not likely to want to share with you in the future.

- **Ask nonjudgmental questions.** Good questions signify that you are interested in what your child is doing, thinking, into. Learn to ask and listen, probe and ask some more. Avoid taking over with mini-lectures and showing off your own knowledge. And avoid being judgmental. No one wants to be asked "What's so cool about . . ." his favorite interest in a critical tone of voice.

E Is for Encouragement

True friends want to see each other succeed. In fact, they help each other succeed. This is actually one of the hidden purposes of friendship—it improves our chances of success in a competitive world. Friends encourage their friends to be their best, make good choices, and focus on their strengths rather than their shortfalls. They are generous with their compliments and stingy with criticism. When they do criticize, it is clear that they mean it to help the friend improve, not to tear the friend down. They are careful not to discourage their friends.

When a child loses courage—when she has become "dis-couraged"— she is more likely to turn to negative behavior to meet her goals. With spirited kids, whose CAPPS behavior is often so disruptive and annoying, it is easy for parents to become harsh, critical, negative, angry, and otherwise discouraging. This just makes the child feel worse about himself and the parent, and leads to more negative behavior. If parent and child were able to put this cycle into words, it might go something like this:

CHILD: "It's my spirited nature to act in ways that bother you."

PARENT: "I get upset when you act in those ways. And I respond by saying critical things in anger."

CHILD: "I feel discouraged by your angry words. This discouragement causes me to misbehave even more."

PARENT: "Your continued misbehavior makes me feel even angrier and frustrated, so I say and use more critical and harsh words."

CHILD: "Stop me if you've heard this before, but I feel discouraged and act out even more when you do."

To break this self-defeating cycle, parents need to do two things. First, they need to learn nondiscouraging methods of discipline (the subject of chapters 6 through 8) and, second, they need to go from being dis-couragers to en-couragers (the subject of chapter 9). In other words, instead of removing courage, we need to use words and actions that instill courage: build them up rather than tear them down. There are a number of ways that parents discourage their children that are also opportunities to encourage them. See which ones apply to you and then think about others that I've missed.

DISCOURAGING	ENCOURAGING
Attacking the child's personality	*Focusing on the child's behavior*
"You are so mean!"	"That really hurts my feelings."
"You're just trying to upset me!"	"I don't like it when you shout inside."
"You are always sticking your nose where it doesn't belong."	"You have a very curious mind."
"Now, be a good girl while I'm gone."	"Be sure to listen to Mrs. Williams while I'm gone."
"You were bad!"	"You had trouble going to bed tonight."
Focusing on mistakes	*Building on strengths*
"You keep knocking over your milk! Be more careful!"	"You haven't spilled your milk all day. Way to go."
"If you don't get into bed this instant, you're going to get a spanking!"	"Nice job brushing your teeth. Now jump into bed so I can continue our story."
"You are always dawdling!"	"Lots of things interest you. Let's be sure to save some time when we get home for you to continue exploring."

DISCOURAGING

Showing a lack of confidence

"This is too hard for you."

"Don't get in to trouble while I'm out."

"You're going to bug me about this all day, aren't you?"

Expecting too much

"Now, sit still and don't move!"

"As smart as you are, there is no reason you can't make all As."

Valuing the child for behavior

"Now, be a big girl and sit still for me."

"Aren't you proud of that medal you won?"

Waiting until she accomplishes something or does something you want and then saying "I love you."

ENCOURAGING

Showing confidence

"Let's take it one step at a time, and you'll be fine."

"I know you can keep calm while I'm out."

"Let's talk about it for five minutes and then make a decision."

Setting realistic goals

"Let's talk about some ways you can calm yourself down when you start to get excited."

"What would you like to improve on in school this semester?"

Valuing the child for herself

"You have a wonderful spirit!"

"I love how you played with such enthusiasm."

Saying "I love you" just because you do.

DISCOURAGING	ENCOURAGING
Using too many negative words, gestures, facial expressions, and tone of voice	*Using more positives*
Words: No, don't, shouldn't, not, bad, stop, why, can't, won't."	Words: Yes, please, thank you, attagirl, attaboy, nice job, keep trying, You can do it, way to go, I appreciate that, Can I help?
Gestures and facial expressions: grimaces, scowls, frowns, angry looks, pointing, shaking a fist, shaking the head.	Gestures and facial expressions: smiles, loving looks, warm glances, encouraging eyes.
Tone: sharp, curt, harsh, angry, disgusted.	Tone: friendly, supportive, firm but caring, calm.

N Is for No

Becoming friends with your child does not mean that you abdicate your role as authority in the family. Sometimes, as I said earlier, even in a peer-peer relationship, one friend must tell another friend no. In a parent-child relationship, this is much more common, and there are many times when the parent must say no to the child.

"No, you can't have another cookie."

"No, you can't stay up any longer."

"No, you may not watch an R-rated movie."

"No, you may not just fast-forward through the 'bad parts.'"

The list is endless. There is no way around the parent's role as limit setter. Some parents try to avoid saying no in an effort to improve the relationship with their children, but the effort usually backfires, as kids who never learn to accept no for an answer grow to be more and more demanding until they find that no one wants to be around them. Spirited kids, who are more persistent (remember that the second *P* in CAPPS is for "persistence"), are inclined to take no as an obstacle to overcome rather than an answer to accept. They will continue to argue, whine, nag, resist, and do whatever else they have found in the past works to either get their way or to at least exhaust the parent. Your job is to stay firm and friendly while maintaining reasonable order in the home. I'll cover a highly effective discipline method in chapter 8, but for now, try these tips to make saying no a little gentler on the relationship:

- **Avoid "hard" no's.** Instead of shouting "No!" or "Stop this instant!" or otherwise getting in the child's face with an angry or harsh command, keep your no's calm and friendly. You aren't the enemy. You are only enforcing the needs of the situation and aren't out to ruin her day. (The exception to this is when a sharply yelled "no" might save a child from impending disaster, such as getting hit by a car.)

- **Pay attention to what your child wants or what is bothering him.** Spirited kids who are hypersensitive may have a legitimate reason for wanting to do something seemingly outrageous. Instead of saying "No, you can't wear that shirt again today" and setting off a tantrum, a little investigation might turn up that this shirt is softer than all his others and doesn't feel scratchy to him. The result might mean buying more shirts of a like material.

- **Acknowledge her feeling or wants verbally.** It feels good to know that someone understands and appreciates our feelings and desires, even if she won't give us what we want. Just saying something like "You really love these cookies, don't you?" is much softer than saying "No, you can't have another cookie."

- **Find a reasonable alternative.** You can follow up your words of empathy and understanding with a decent alternative that will help solve the problem without violating your own values or the needs of the situation. "I wish I could let you have more cookies, but too much sugar isn't good for you. How about a nice, juicy carrot instead?" Well, you probably figured out that this alternative pretty much sucks! That's because I can't think of a decent alternative to a cookie that isn't also sweet. When you can't think of one either, you might try the next tip instead . . .

- **Grant them their wish as fantasy.** This method, created by the late child psychologist Chaim Ginott, is great with younger kids. It not only lets them know that you are on their side but often seems to satisfy their desires. For example, "You really love these cookies, don't you? I bet you wish we could eat cookies three meals a day and then for dessert have more cookies! Maybe your bed could be made of cookies, so that when you woke up in the night and wanted a cookie, you could just take a big bite!"

D Is for Delight

There are very few silver bullets in the parenting business, but if I've found one that almost always serves to improve the parent-child relationship, it is this: Find something about your child that delights you and watch the child improve. It's a small miracle, but when we really find something in our children that we especially like, the relationship takes a huge leap forward. With our son, Ben, it was always his sense of humor. His quick wit and ready smile were, in fact, delightful. Enjoying that humor was a gift for the entire family, one that we always tried to encourage.

Friends enjoy each other and delight in the special qualities that make each person unique. It makes them feel good, and it makes the friend feel delightful. That's good for self-esteem, confidence, and the overall relationship. What about your child delights you? You may need to look closely, but when you find it, you will soon find another and another.

The reason this book is about taming children and not breaking them is that our aim is to protect these special qualities in our children that will serve them well in the future and bring joy to themselves and others. Harshly breaking the child's will or spirit would likely do damage to this element of delight for all time. Ben, now fourteen, just put together his first stand-up comedy performance for his school's year-end talent show. Parents were not allowed to attend, but I hear he was a big hit.

The Dynamics of Power

*The miracle, or the power, that elevates the few is to be found in
their industry, application, and perseverance under the promptings
of a brave, determined spirit.*

—MARK TWAIN (1835–1910)

WHEN THREE-YEAR-OLD NICOLAS refused to put on his socks,
and his mother became angry, he did not give in. Instead, he refused.
He cried. He yelled. When she called his father into the room, she
thought this macho military man would lay down the law, and
Nicolas would knuckle under. Instead, Nicolas refused. He cried.
He yelled. And the more his parents commanded, threatened, and
cajoled, the more Nicolas rebelled. Nothing worked, and the socks
did not go on.

Anyone who has ever parented, taught, or otherwise been in a
position of leadership with a spirited child knows the frustration
of locking horns in a power struggle with one of these amazingly
powerful young people. When a spirited child's power (the first *P* in
CAPPS) is triggered, the effect is multiplied by his second *P* of persistence. This P^2 phenomena is not unlike Einstein's famous $E = mc^2$,
in that it creates a tremendous amount of energy. Power struggles
with spirited children can therefore last for hours, often exhausting
the parents and leaving the entire family reeling.

When ten-year-old Elena wanted her mom to take her to the mall,
and her mom refused, saying that she was too busy, Elena did not take

no for an answer. She whined. She pleaded. She yelled. Eventually her mother wore down and promised to take her if Elena would just keep quiet for fifteen minutes so that she could get some work done. Elena gave her ten minutes, and a grateful mom took her to the mall.

If there is one quality that separates spirited kids from other kids the most, it is power. Yes, they are also curious, adventurous, persistent, and sensitive, but the quality that most drives parents up the proverbial wall is power. These kids want what they want, and they have the energy to either get it or to at least make you miserable for denying them what they want. This is not the real problem, however. Power, whether it be for running a computer, winning a horse race, or getting a ride to the mall, is a necessary thing. Everybody wants power. The problem comes when parents do not understand how to deal with their spirited child's excessive desire for power, and instead of making the situation better, add gas to a burning fire. This chapter will hopefully give you some new ideas about the dynamics of power so that you don't fall into the trap of making a bad situation worse. Then, in chapters 6 through 8 on discipline, I'll share some effective methods of handling misbehavior with spirited, powerful children.

It is my experience that the following six principles of power apply to all people, whether organized as nations, companies, families, or otherwise. For the purposes of this book, however, we are obviously interested in how they apply to spirited children.

Principles of Power

Principle 1:
All humans Want Power (1A: Power Is Morally Neutral)

Power is neither good nor bad. It is simply the energy required to get something done. Whether that something is building a bridge or blowing up a bridge does not matter to the concept of power. Whether building a bridge or blowing up a bridge is a good or bad thing is also besides the point to power. Power only cares about there being sufficient energy and capability to make it happen.

This desire to make things happen—to be powerful—is a natural desire of all human beings. From the time we first cry because we are hungry and discover that crying makes food mysteriously appear, we continue to want more and more power to make things happen. We eventually learn that depending on others to do things for us is a risky business, so most people progress to developing the skills to get things done themselves. "Look what I did, Mommy!" becomes the new cry of the young child as she learns to own her personal power. Learning, skill building, problem solving—these are all aspects of power that successful children develop on their own and in conjunction with parents, teachers, peers, and others. In a perfect world, say the Garden of Eden, such power would not be necessary, as everything would be provided. In our world, however, power is a cornerstone of survival and success. But how that power is used can be for better or for worse.

Children who grow up with a good sense of courage and self-esteem while receiving effective guidance from parents and others learn to use their power for useful purposes. They learn how to give and take, share, postpone gratification, take turns, tolerate frustration, and otherwise modulate their power within the context of the situation. They don't scream and yell for a cookie when told it is too close to dinner. They wait until after dinner for their cookie. On the other hand, there are kids who have not learned these lessons in self-control who face frustrations with anger and outrage, who storm against the limits imposed by others and seek to overpower all who stand in their way.

Some of these kids are the spirited children of this book. These are not malicious children who seek power as bullies seek power to control others for ego gratification. More often they suffer from intense frustrations of their own, often caused by their personal CAPPS: extreme curiosity ("I didn't come in when you called because I was too interested in what I was doing"); heightened need for adventure ("I won't go to bed because I might miss something!"); persistence ("I just *can't* take no for an answer!"), and sensitivity ("I don't want to put on these socks because they are too scratchy!"). These qualities often put spirited children into conflict with parents, teachers, and others who are invested in teaching them to live in harmony with others. When these authority figures use power tactics of their own to control these children, a conflict easily escalates into a full-fledged power struggle, with each side attempting to overpower the other. The result is usually a very frustrated adult and a sobbing child who doesn't understand what's happening to him.

The goal of this book is not to diminish a spirited child's power but to help him learn to use his power for the good of himself and others. When directed properly, this power is a force to cherish, not resist.

Principle 2:
Some People Pursue Power for Power Itself

Most people want power as a necessary means to achieve their goals, to make the things they want to happen occur. Children also operate according to goals. However, most parents never stop to think about what their child's goal actually is. In fact, most people mistakenly believe that children behave according to causes. They spend their energy thinking about what caused this or that misbehavior. Was the misbehavior "caused" by too little sleep, too much sugar, a mean word by a peer, lack of time with a parent, bad genes, bad environment, bad divorce, or bad breath? The list is endless. And though some of these factors might contribute to misbehavior, it is much more useful to think about the child's goals for the future rather than causes in the past.

The central question to ask with any misbehavior is: "What is this person hoping to accomplish with this behavior? What is his goal?" Sometimes the goal will be obvious to both the parent and the child. For example, the child may want a cookie, to stay up later, to avoid a bath, or any other obvious activity or object. But in addition to the obvious goal, people usually have psychological goals of which they are not even aware. For example, a child's misbehavior will often be aimed at one of four common goals: (1) getting contact with an adult, (2) protecting his own safety or self-esteem, (3) avoiding a difficult task, or (4) gaining power.

It is this goal of power that is relevant to managing spirited children. They have it. They like it. They want more of it. When power itself becomes the goal rather than the results that power can achieve, struggles for power emerge on a regular basis. The fight is no longer about having the cookie but about being in control.

There are two clues that tell us when a child's goal has become gaining power over others. The first is the feeling that it produces in the object of that power play. Whether a parent, a teacher, or someone else, the feeling is usually one of anger. We become frustrated by the child's refusal to cooperate with us or by his demands that we obey him. It is as if the child is saying to himself, "I count only when I'm bossing her around or showing her that she can't boss me around." The parent's own frustration, when not handled effectively, easily mushrooms into anger. And once the parent becomes angry, the child has won the struggle. How has the child won when the parent doesn't give in to the unreasonable demands? Because the very act of losing our temper says to the power-driven child, "Look how powerful you are: You made me angry!" For a child to be able to control the emotions of a giant in his world is powerful stuff. You lose your temper, you lose.

The second clue that a child is pursuing power for power itself is how he responds to our attempts to correct his misbehavior. With most goals, when a child is corrected, he will stop the misbehavior. But with a powerful child, our correction is often taken as a challenge that just fuels further misbehavior. The more we fight, the more he continues to misbehave or rebel. It becomes like Marlon Brando's famous line from the movie *The Wild One*: "What are you rebelling against, Johnny?" To which Brando (as motorcycle gang leader Johnny Strabler) answers, "Whaddya got?" In other words, "It doesn't matter. I'm just rebelling for the sake of power—to show you that I can't be bossed around."

Principle 3:
The Person in Position to Say No Is in the More Powerful Position

The power generated by an act of rebellion is learned very early in life. We want something, and a parent says no. We reach for something, and a parent moves our hand away and says no. We go to put something in our mouth, and, again, that ubiquitous giant takes it away and says no. We absorb this information, and then one day when the unsuspecting giant tells us to do something we don't want to do, we take on his stern tone of voice and say firmly, "No! Right back at you, big guy!" (Well, we say, the no part, anyway.) And then we learn an even more important lesson: Parents can't really make us do as much as they think they can! If we can say no to their demand that we take a bath, go to bed, stop playing with our food, quit picking our nose—you name it—then they really can't make us do it. They can yell and scream, make a real nuisance of themselves, even hurt us for not doing it. But unless they physically move us, they can't really make us. The person in the position to say no has a lot of power.

Fortunately, this principle cuts both ways. When we as parents are in a position to say no, we hold the cards. When a child demands to be taken to the mall "right now!" we have the power to say no.

When he wants us to get him a cookie, and only we can reach it or know where we hide them, we have a lot of power. Using our power to say no is one way that parents can set limits with spirited children. Of course, when we say no, and then they "yell and scream and make a real nuisance of themselves," and then we give in and do what they demanded, we have just taught them to do the same in the future. After all, if it works, then it is a successful power tactic. And spirited kids, as I've been saying, are into power. So be careful that when you say no, you really mean it. And then change your mind only when your child approaches you with a respectful argument and not a lot of sound and fury. In chapter 8, I'll also show you a good method for saying no in a way that improves the prospect of your child accepting your no without an emotional meltdown or tantrum.

When your child is in position to say no, you still have a responsibility as a parent to manage the situation. This means finding creative ways to get the child to say yes. And by creative, I don't mean threats, punishments, yelling, or other old-school forms of discipline. Neither do I mean giving in. I'll suggest some of these creative measures in the next section of this chapter and in chapters 6, 7, and 8.

Principle 4:
Power Can Be Achieved through Either Positive or Negative Behavior

Because power is neutral, it may be achieved through either more or less positive or negative behavior. Spirited children have more natural power than other kids, but how they use this power can be directed toward positive behavior or negative behavior. A child who wants to exercise his power will easily rebel against a parent who is always giving orders and trying to dictate his life to him. However, when we learn to work with the child and allow him to participate in decisions that affect his life, he gains legitimate power and does not need to resort to rebellion.

Our job as a leader of children is to help them choose to use their power in useful ways and be respectful of others. We can redirect their misbehavior toward positive ways to achieve power. For example, a spirited child who refuses to take a bath, and gains power over his pleading parents in the process, can be given legitimate power by asking him how he would like to get clean and when? Enlisting his help in solving the problem is empowering. It says that his opinions and solutions matter. It says to him that he does not need to rebel in order to have influence around here. It says that we are not the enemy but an ally who wants to help him solve problems. It says that he is powerful when using his mind to solve problems.

As I've said, it is far easier to achieve power by rebelling than any other way. All you have to do is say no. In fact, you don't even have to *say* no. All you really have to do is not comply. Kids will often rebel silently against their parents by simply not doing what we ask them to do. Such power struggles can often be very quiet. And if a child feels that his parent is too powerful to fight head-on, the child can always strike a blow in the power struggle by failing. Since it is our goal to see kids succeed, they can show us that we can't boss them around by failing. And since they know our value systems inside out, they will often choose to fail in our favorite ones. For example, if you value education, your kids can defeat you by doing poorly in school. It is as if they are saying, "OK, you can make me go to school, but you can't make me learn!" Of course, they are not consciously aware of this goal, but it governs their behavior accordingly nonetheless.

Principle 5:
The Use of Force Often Increases Resistance

There is an activity we have parents do in our *Active Parenting* courses that you can replicate on your own. Find an adult partner and stand face-to-face. Press your palms against each other lightly about chest high. Then, without giving any instructions, begin to push against your partner. You will notice that he pushes back. Push harder and see what happens. Chances are that your partner will push back harder. Increase your force, and he will continue to increase his resistance. Now stop pushing and see what he does. He will stop pushing also. In fact, if you stop pushing abruptly, he will likely lose his balance and fall forward.

Why the resistance when pushed against? Most people do not like to be pushed around, so they naturally push back when imposed upon. Spirited children are even more likely than most to push back, since their goal of power is so prominent. Unfortunately, old-school parenting teaches that when a little force does not work with a child, use more force. While this may work with some kids, it is almost guaranteed to make the problem worse with a spirited child. The more force that is used, the more Seabiscuit strains against the ropes and rears, kicking at his handlers. Even when you actually use enough force to subdue a spirited child, the victory is only temporary. The child signals a retreat so that he can live to fight another day. Without establishing human ties with the child—taming him—force will usually just increase the resistance.

In order to decrease the child's resistance, first you have to stop pushing. The warrior parent says, "You'll get in that bath this minute, or you'll wish you had!" And the child resists. "No!" And because the person in position to say no is in the more powerful position, the child usually wins. However, less force paradoxically becomes more power. If you stop pushing, your child has nothing to push back against and loses his balance. It then becomes possible for you to suggest an alternative solution. "I'm not going to fight with you about taking a bath. But I do love you and want you to be healthy, so how do you suggest that we keep you clean and healthy?" This is not the language or attitude of war. This is a peacemaker talking. The war is over, so now what are we going to do? Resistance is futile, because no one is attacking or angry. We may as well figure out a solution to the problem.

Principle 5A:
The More You Try to Control Another Person, the Less You Can Influence That Person

There is a mistaken belief among parents and those who are annoyed by disruptive children that parents should "control" their child. The reason that this is a mistaken belief is *not* because disruptive children should be allowed to run free in public places or otherwise disturb the sanity of grown-ups. Kids need to be taught manners, respect, and other lessons of group living. The mistake is to believe that one person can control another person. Except where physical force is used—and there are certainly instances where force is a legitimate strategy (for example, when a police officer subdues a felon, or a parent removes a screaming two-year-old from a restaurant)—people do not control others, they influence them.

The word *influence* indicates that the control still rests with the other person. Instead of trying to control another's behavior, we are better off trying to influence her thinking so that she chooses a different course of behavior. The actual choice (that is, control), however, is still in the person's own hands. The paradox is that the more we try to control a rebellious person, the more he resists our influence. As children get older, and physical control becomes less and less possible, this influence is more and more important. Parents who rely on force and control while kids are young often find themselves in terrible power struggles that they cannot win as their children grow into the teen years. Parents who have developed respectful relationships with their children, on the other hand, find that they still have a lot of influence with their teens when the time comes.

Principle 6:
People Will Often Accept the Perception of Power in Place of Real Power

The origins of power lie deep in our primitive past and are closely tied to the drive to survive on a hostile planet. Those with the power to make things happen, whether it was discovering fire or killing a saber-toothed tiger, were more likely to survive. They were also more likely to increase the clan's chances of survival. These people developed a certain prestige in their society as powerful members who were accorded respect—and maybe the best skin in the cave for sleeping. We still respect powerful people in our modern society, not so much for survival but because they can increase or decrease the quality of our lives through their use of power. We often still pay them increased respect and afford them special privileges. This respect for power transaction has gone on for so long that people want to be considered powerful—not just for what they can accomplish with their power but for the status of power itself. Power in our contemporary society is more often about ego than the results real power can actually accomplish. We want to *feel* powerful, even when we cannot make things happen our way. Conversely, feeling powerless creates a sense of frustration and rebelliousness in people.

Giving a spirited child enough power to *feel* powerful is therefore essential in helping to tame his powerful will. This is why parents who attempt to break their child's will usually wind up actually fueling the power struggle. You don't need to give your child his way, but you do need to give him his power. Instead of trying to subdue the child, parents can learn to share power within limits that are reasonable for the situation. Instead of a win-lose power struggle, parents can focus on solving the problem at hand. Involving the child as a collaborator in finding a solution opens up the immense doors of cooperation. The following ten tactics for avoiding or defusing power struggles will suggest ways to do this.

Ten Tactics for Avoiding (or Defusing) Power Struggles

Tactic 1: Don't Fight and Don't Give In

This first guideline is also the most important. The key to getting out of a power struggle or avoiding one to begin with is to neither allow yourself to get pulled into a fight with a spirited child nor give in to her unreasonable demands. Parents almost always err in one of these two directions. Old-school parents believe they have to show the child who is boss and so get hooked into trying to overpower the child with anger, threats, punishment, and the like. As we saw in the earlier section on principles of power, this just leads the child to resist more furiously in order not to be overpowered. Permissive parents, on the other hand, attempt to avoid the power struggle by appeasing the child and giving in. This strategy also backfires, as the child learns that her displays of power get her what she wants. Many a spirited child has also become a spoiled child in the process.

How do you avoid fighting without giving in? First, you have to summon your own power. You are the leader in the family, and you need to embrace that role with courage and confidence. You have the right, and the responsibility, to make decisions that affect your child's health, safety, and character. You also have the power to make these decisions happen. Don't be afraid to exercise this power in the best interest of your child, your family, and your community. Notice your tone of voice, your body language, your facial expression, as well as your words. All should say very clearly, "I love you, I respect you, I want your input. But the bottom line is that I'm the parent, and I'll make the final decision about this."

Your child will test you to see if you will stand firm, fold, or fight. If he cannot get you to give in, then getting you into a fight is the next best thing. You have to be willing to absorb his anger and defiance without being provoked into a fight. If you fight, you lose. Instead, use the guidelines covered in this section (and in chapter 10 on handling tantrums) to defuse your child's anger. When necessary, use the discipline skills in the next chapters to reinforce the lesson you want to teach. Remember, your goal is not to win a battle or keep the peace. Your goal is to tame your spirited child over time. Refusing to fight or give in is a key step in this process of establishing ties.

Tactic 2: Give Choices, Not Orders

Modern children are more sensitive to orders than previous generations, and spirited children, who by nature are even more sensitive and more powerful, are even more so.

The fact is that very few of us really like to be bossed around. We would much prefer to be asked politely to do something, or even better, to be given some real power. Real power comes by way of choice. When we have options in our lives, we feel empowered rather than controlled. Our desire to resist is mysteriously reduced as we weigh these options and decide. In fact, choice is often an illusion that carries with it very little real power. But as I explained in power principle 6, people are often satisfied with the perception of power when they do not have actual power.

I realize that this sounds a bit Machiavellian. Am I suggesting that we manipulate spirited children with false power, smoke, and mirrors? Should we lead them to think they have power that they do not? And if we do, won't this come back to haunt us someday when they figure out they have been duped? The answer is that we do give them real power, but within the limits that we think appropriate for the situation. Like a horse tamer gives a wild horse the freedom to choose where to graze, as long as he chooses within the fenced-in area, freedom within limits is both empowering and limiting at the same time. It says to the child, "You have *some* power, even as you recognize that there are limits to this power."

Children eventually come to love this arrangement, as it provides security in knowing that they are safely within borders patrolled by a loving and fair parent and yet free to exercise their desires within those borders. As they gain experience and maturity, the limits are expanded, and the child is allowed to make more and more of his own decisions. Eventually he has the same freedom within limits that are afforded to all of us in this "free" country. Because, after all, isn't our own freedom partly an illusion? Aren't we limited by laws and the needs of others? And yet mature adults do not mind this, as we also value the security that comes with giving up some of our freedom—but not all of it.

Let's look at a practical example of giving spirited children choices rather than orders:

Order

PARENT: "Stop playing with that game and come to dinner!"
CHILD: "In a minute!"
PARENT: "Stop playing and come to the table this instant!"

Choice

PARENT: "Do you want to come to the table now, or do you need five minutes to wind up what you are doing?"

Notice that the order says, "What you want is of no importance. Only what I want really matters here. You have no power in this situation. I have all of the power. If you want any power, you have to rebel to get it, since I have left you no other option."

On the other hand, the choice says, "I understand that you have needs, too. One of those needs may be some transition time from moving from one activity to another [especially important for spirited kids, as they are naturally more persistent—remember?] I also understand that you have a need for power and don't like feeling taken for granted. You can exercise that power by choosing to come to dinner now or by waiting for a few minutes. You don't have to say no in order to gain this power. All you have to do is choose."

No single method works in every situation, and there will be times when giving a choice still results in the child saying no. When that happens, choices can be combined with logically connected consequences for a respectful form of discipline that will often get results. This method of "logical consequences" is presented in chapter 7.

The beauty of choices, however, is that it gives the child legitimate power, while the only way for a child who receives an order to exercise his power is by refusing to follow the order. This gives him power by the easiest means possible: rebellion. While there are certainly times when kids need a swift order, especially when safety is an issue, there are many more times when a choice can be given within limits that are still acceptable to the parent. Try some of these choices instead of issuing orders:

- "Do you want to do your homework before dinner or afterward?"
- "Would you rather have broccoli or string beans tonight with dinner?"
- "Would you rather set the table or take out the trash?"
- "Which of your books would you like me to read to you tonight?"
- "Why don't you go with me to the grocery store so that you can pick out some of your favorite foods?" (You will want to limit choices to foods that are OK with you.)
- "Which jacket do you want to wear: the brown one or this blue one?"

Tactic 3: Motivate Your Child with When-Then Scenarios

Most people, spirited children included, would rather do what they want to do rather than what they need to do. Said another way, we'd rather play than work. Unfortunately, Adam and Eve blew it, and we find ourselves living in a world that demands work. Part of maturity is accepting this reality and adopting a "work before play" philosophy of life. Teaching children to fulfill their obligations before doing the fun things in life is a valuable lesson. It's also a way out of power struggles.

When you find yourself in a situation where you want your child to do something, and she is avoiding or refusing to comply, using a when-then scenario can often motivate her to do what is required. Rather than fighting or giving in, simply think of something that she likes doing to connect with the thing that you want her to do. For example, if you want her to clean up her room, but she would rather watch TV, you might say, "Honey, when you have cleaned up your room, then you may watch TV." Notice that this is not a bribe. You aren't coming up with something out of the ordinary as a reward, but rather taking two events that occur anyway and sequencing them so that the work comes before the play. Bribes often take the form of "if you . . ." rather than "when you . . ." and should be avoided. Once you start rewarding kids for positive behavior, there is no end to it. Being smart little capitalists, they will milk you for more and more. Instead of learning to cooperate, they learn to manipulate.

When-then scenarios do not reward, they order. And they can bring order to your family. Another name, by the way, for this sophisticated psychological method is "Grandma's rule," because by the time you become a grandma or grandpa, you've figured this out for yourself. Take a look at these examples and see how you can use Grandma to help you avoid power struggles without fighting or giving in:

- "When you have washed the dishes, you may go outside and play."
- "When you have done your homework, you may play on the computer for a half hour."
- "When you are ready for school, then you can have break-fast."
- "When I'm finished cleaning up in here, then I'll read you a story."
- "When you calm down, then we'll talk about what you want calmly."

Tactic 4: Stay Firm and Friendly

Whether you thought Ronald Reagan was great president or a great mistake, you have to admit one thing about the man as a leader. He projected himself as a benevolent father figure who stood firm and friendly in a perilous world. When dealing with power struggles, whether with the Soviet Union in Reagan's time or with a spirited child in your own time, it pays to remain firm and friendly. (However, I don't recommend that you follow Reagan's lead and refer to your children as "the evil empire"!)

The point is to project strength without becoming aggressive and to project friendliness without becoming a doormat. Keep your tone of voice calm but very much in charge. The message you want to project in your tone of voice and body language is that you are a friendly superpower. Remember that your goal, like the U.S.'s goal during the Cold War, is to neither fight nor give in. The friendliness in your voice says that you do not want to fight, but the firmness says that you have no need to give in, either. You can work it out peacefully, but you will not be taken advantage of. And most important, you are a friend and not an enemy.

Tactic 5: Ask for What You Want Respectfully

Think of a time when somebody in your life asked you to do something disrespectfully. Maybe it was a tone of voice barking at you. Maybe it was the condescending way you were addressed. Maybe it was a look in the eye, or even a lack of eye contact altogether. Whatever the disrespect, I'm guessing that you did not feel very good about meeting the person's request (or demand). You may have gone along anyway, but something in the relationship was damaged, and at some point this damage came back to haunt the relationship. Maybe it was a store that you never went back to. Maybe it was a supervisor who led you to resign. Maybe it was a parent you found ways to get even with through future misbehavior.

The fact is that in our egalitarian society, where everyone wants to be treated as equal, respect is a cornerstone of healthy relationships. Children are no exception. They seem to know through osmosis that they are entitled to be treated respectfully—just like everyone else. When parents put them down, use a contemptuous tone of voice, ignore their wants and point of view, and otherwise show them disrespect, they no longer accept it as their lot in life. Today's children, and particularly today's spirited children, react with resentment, and whether they show it immediately or in the future, they will find ways to get even.

This creates a bind for a parent in a power struggle. The child has been misbehaving. You are feeling frustrated and angry, and have had it up to here! And now I'm telling you that you have to be respectful of this willful child who has been anything but respectful to you? I must be crazy! Yes, crazy like a fox. The fact is that when you treat with respect someone who is treating you disrespectfully, you hold up a mirror to that person, and he sees in your calm, respectful reflection his exaggerated behavior, and something inside him wants to change to match yours. Well, OK, not always.

But the alternative, asking for what you want disrespectfully, is like throwing gas on a fire.

Tactic 6: Avoid Character Attacks or Other Methods Designed to Hurt or Shame the Child into Cooperating

There are a surprising number of people who seem to have missed the old expression that "you can catch more bees with honey than with vinegar." These people go about trying to solve problems by insulting, complaining, criticizing, and even shaming and humiliating the person they want to change. Then they are surprised when they do not get the change they want. Many of these people are parents.

Imagine a mother coming into a room where her five-year-old child is happily finger painting the bathroom floor with about fifty dollars' worth of Mom's cosmetics. She flies into a rage, shouting, "What do you think you are doing?! You know better than to get into stuff that doesn't belong to you! Look at this mess! You should be ashamed of yourself! This stuff costs money, you know! Now, go to your room and think about what you have done!" (Followed by a swift spank on the bottom and a lot of crying.)

The child runs to his room and buries his head in his pillow, sobbing pitifully. My question to you is, what is he thinking (either consciously or subconsciously)?

(A) "You know, Mom is right. I really should know better. I'm glad she loves me enough to let me know when I'm getting out of line. From now on, I resolve to do better. I'll show her that I can be a child she will be proud of, and I'll start by repaying her for the damage I did to her cosmetics."

(B) "She's mean! I hate her! Maybe she's too big to fight head-on, but I have my ways, and I'll show her she can't treat me like this!"

As much as we might wish for response *A*, the chances are that the "I hate you!" response is more often what is triggered by such parental attacks. I do realize that some kids will knuckle under and feel ashamed by such a parental outburst. They may even try to do better in the future or at least keep out of harm's way (sadly, their parent's way!). They will also grow up to lead lives of quiet desperation, never knowing why they never feel very good about themselves or anyone else. Lucky for you that spirited children aren't likely to fall into this category. They are more likely to fight such mistreatment tooth and nail, redoubling their efforts to exert their own power in a fight to the death—and since you are older, it usually means that you die first, and they finally win.

Let's look at this from another perspective: Are you aware that most football coaches will talk up the opposition before a game and avoid at all cost putting them down? It does not matter if their team is a thirty-point favorite and the other team hasn't won a game all season; to hear the coach talk, you would think that the opponent was just a break or two away from the national championship! Why do coaches do this? Because they know that when weaker teams (or individuals) are insulted by stronger ones, they become stronger themselves just to show the arrogant #$%&** that they will not be talked about disrespectfully. Smart coaches do not want this added motivation in their opponents' minds on game day, so they emphasize the positive.

Smart parents also know that it is essential to refrain from attacking a child either physically or verbally as a way of expressing anger or disciplining misbehavior. We will talk more about anger in chapter 10, but for now just be sure that it does not lead you to indulge in character attacks, shaming, or other forms of abuse. Otherwise, your child will just redouble his power efforts to defeat you.

Tactic 7: Take Your Sail out of Your Child's Wind

Have you ever tried to sail a boat into the teeth of a hurricane? Me neither. In fact, I have no fear of perfect storms or any other kind of treacherous weather, because at the first sign of high winds, I'd get my sailboat back to shore and get a nice cup of hot tea. Not very macho, I know. But as the Hungarian philosopher Zsa Zsa Gabor once said, "Macho isn't mucho." And I bet that you are smart enough to join me. In fact, if you saw the movie *The Perfect Storm,* you were probably like me in thinking, "Turn the blasted boat around already and get home! There is a huge storm coming! The fish will be there another day! Ahhh . . . too late."

Yet when it comes to raising children, even spirited children, parents seem to think that they should meet the challenge head-on and drive their little boat up the crest of a thirty-foot wave into the teeth of the storm. The next thing you know, the boat has capsized, and everyone is gasping for air below deck in a water-filled cabin, wondering what happened. A better strategy when a spirited child tries to engage you in a power struggle is to *take your sail out of his wind*. In other words, remove yourself from the situation. "But no-ooooooooo," the American philosopher Steve Martin would say, you have to prove to your child that you are the boss and take the wind out of *his* sails. So you argue, threaten, punish, scream, and otherwise engage in a power struggle. The result is that he wins even when he loses, because he has succeeded in bringing you down to his level.

Instead of trying to change him, it is much easier to change yourself. Stay calm and use one of the discipline skills in chapters 6 through 8. Or if he continues to blow hurricanelike in your direction, simply excuse yourself to go to the bathroom. This "bathroom technique," as psychiatrist Rudolf Dreikurs once called it, works wonders. It provides a reasonable way for you to extricate yourself from the power struggle, thus leaving him to huff and puff without a sail to inflate. When you take your sail out of his wind, the storm often loses power very rapidly. (And by the way, while in the bathroom, you might want to reread chapters 6 through 8 for some ideas about what to do when you come out!) With young children, who cannot be left alone without danger to themselves or the furniture, you will need to put them in a crib or other safe place before excusing yourself.

Tactic 8: Put Yourself in Your Child's Shoes

When most people become engaged in a power struggle, they revert to a competitive sports model. In other words, if you win, then I lose, and vice versa. The win-lose model does govern sports competition, but in most other human endeavors there is room for multiple winners (and unfortunately, multiple losers, with no winners). Take a business competition, for example. Hertz and Avis were number one and number two in rental car sales for years. Avis even built its advertising campaign around the slogan "We try harder"—because it was second to Hertz. Who won this competition? They both did. As they focused attention on their rivalry, profits soared for both companies.

One way to sidestep a power struggle is to look for ways for both you and your opponent to come out winners. This is possible because very often the two of you have different goals that are not in conflict. Rather than assume that the other party wants exactly the same thing as you, put yourself in his shoes and see what else he might want that you can give him without sacrificing your own goals. You would be surprised how often you can both win when you take the time to see it from the other person's perspective. Spirited children are no exception. What they often *really* want may be different from what you think they want. You may be trying to get them to do their homework while they protest that they will do it later. You may feel like you have to get them doing it "right now because I said so," or else they win and you lose. But it isn't really about winning and losing. It's about getting the homework done. What they really want may be to have more say about *when* the homework gets done. What you want is to make sure that they do their homework before bedtime. This leaves room for a win-win. By asking your child, "When would you like to do your homework?" you give her the power that she wants without sacrificing your own goals or abdicating your position as family leader.

What if she chooses to do her homework an hour before bedtime? Let her try it. If she gets too tired or does not have time to finish, then you can politely say, "I guess we'll have to pick an earlier time tomorrow." There is no need to get angry, just help her learn from the experience and then stay firm about picking an earlier time the next day.

Tactic 9: Acknowledge the Legitimacy of Your Child's Wishes

Putting yourself in your child's shoes can help you understand what she really wants. She can't always *have* what she wants, but by letting her know that you understand her wishes and respect them, she is much more likely to accept no for an answer. Let's face it, nobody likes to be shot down, and spirited kids like it a lot less than anybody. If your child doesn't want to wear the shirt you've laid out for him, which of these responses are likely to fuel a power struggle and which are likely to ease it?

1. "Stop this nonsense and put on your shirt this minute!"
2. "Why are you making such a big deal out of a lousy shirt?!"
3. "You must really not like wearing this shirt, huh?"
4. "I'm going to count to three, and if that shirt is not on, you are going right to bed after dinner tonight. Do you understand me?"
5. "Sometimes you wish that you didn't have to wear shirts at all, don't you? Well, I sometimes feel that way about shoes!"

It isn't hard to imagine which responses you would prefer to hear if you were the child in the above scenarios. The in-your-face responses (1, 2, and 4) to a spirited child are a direct challenge to his sense of power. You might as well challenge him to a David and Goliath duel at dawn, and we know how that one turned out for the big guy. On the other hand, the empathetic responses (3 and 5) are actually disarming. They say, "I understand. I care. I'm on your side here. I'm your friend, not your enemy." This opens the door to real cooperation and problem solving.

Acknowledging the legitimacy of your spirited child's feelings and wishes also accomplishes something almost magical inside her brain. While it does not give the child what she wants in reality, it may give it to her in her *imagination*. Often, this is enough to reset the chemical imbalance in her brain so that an emotional storm is averted or reduced. Think about the following scenes and how acknowledging the child's wishes might have this assuaging effect:

Scene 1. Reality

CHILD: "I don't want to go to school today."
PARENT: "I'm sorry, but we all have our jobs to do, and yours is to go to school."
CHILD: "No! I don't want to!"
PARENT: "We all have to do things we don't want to do sometimes."
CHILD: "No! You can't make me!"

Scene 1. Wish Acknowledgement

CHILD: "I don't want to go to school today."
PARENT: "I bet you wish there were a big snowstorm, and all the schools closed down today, so we could stay home and play all day."

CHILD: "Yes! That would be so cool!"

PARENT: "Wouldn't it! I wish I could call my boss and tell her that I'm not coming in today and instead stay here with you and bake cookies."

CHILD: "Big ones, with chocolate chips!"

PARENT: "By the dozen!"

CHILD: "We could fill up the whole kitchen with them!"

PARENT: "Billions and billions of cookies."

In the first scene, the parent sticks to reality and escalates the power struggle. While her words are completely reasonable, to a spirited child they are cold and heartless and worthy of a fight. In the second scene, the parent understands that the child already knows that she has to go to school. So instead of lecturing her on her responsibilities, she joins her in a little wish fulfillment. The result is a mood shift that changes the dynamics from a power struggle to a creative collaboration.

Tactic 10: Do the Unexpected

People in power struggles are pretty predictable. A little power doesn't work, so they use more. The other person responds to this "more" by increasing his own power tactics. Pretty soon a conflict has escalated into another full-fledged battle. In fact, because kids know what to expect from us once they push our hot button, they know how to engage us until we either give in or give them a full fight. And remember, if we either fight or give in, they win. Of course, this usually happens at a subconscious level, with neither the child nor the parent knowing why he is yelling and angry. Both parent and child have been conditioned to react in these predictable, if destructive, cycles, almost as if swept along by a storm of emotion. To break these negative cycles, you can often do the unexpected and shift the child's subconscious expectation. For example:

Mother was tired of reminding ten-year-old Austin of his job to set the table before dinner. It seemed that every evening the family would be ready to sit down at the table, but there was no Austin. She'd have to call him several times before he'd come, by which time she was angry and ready for a confrontation. These power struggles often ended with an unpleasant meal for everyone. One day she decided to try something she had seen on a parenting video. She told Austin that tonight she would not remind him at all. He was to have the table set by 6:00 and she was confident that he could handle this responsibility.

At 6:10, Austin came sauntering into the kitchen to set the table, as Mother was draining the hot water from the spaghetti. As he began to set the table, Mother said, "No, Austin. You were to have the table set by 6:00, and it's now 6:10. So just have a seat with the others." As Father and the rest of the family took their seats at the bare table, Austin slid into his place. Mother, with no show of emotion, began serving the spaghetti on the bare table in front of each family member. If you think this was bad, you should have been there when she began serving the sauce!

Serving spaghetti on a bare table may not be your cup of tea for a power-struggle intervention, but it was unexpected, and as such, had the effect of snapping Austin out of his complacency regarding his chore of setting the table. You can believe that the next night he was setting the table by 5:45. Another form of doing the unexpected can be the wish fulfillment discussed in tactic 9. When kids expect us to get angry, threaten to punish, or otherwise behave in an autocratic fashion, and instead we show genuine concern for their feelings and desires, it creates an unexpected shock to the dynamics of the situation. It is as if the subconscious mind were saying, "Hey, wait a minute! I thought you were the enemy. You are acting more like a friend. How can I stay mad at you?"

Likewise, when a parent who more often gives in, acting like a doormat to her child, decides to stay firm ("I'm sorry, Karen, I know that cookie looks good, but it's too close to dinner. You may have one for dessert later"), the parent-child dynamics are also sent into an unexpected shock. "What's going on here?" the child wonders. "I thought she would do anything to avoid a confrontation. Maybe I've underestimated the woman."

Finally, parents can do the unexpected by asking the child to help solve the problem. When kids are shown the respect of being included in the process of finding solutions, their mental and emotional energy can be redirected toward useful activities instead of power struggles. "I know you really want to spend the night at TJ's house this Friday, but we have all been invited over to Aunt Lisa's. Is there any way to work it out so that everyone feels good about the evening?" Of course, there may not be an alternative that *really* works for everyone, but the mere process of inviting the child to help find a solution is often enough to diffuse the power struggle. We will see how this process of finding alternatives can be fused with discipline skills in chapter 8 for some very effective results.

Discipline: Showdown at the OK Corral

Home is the place where boys and girls first learn how to limit their wishes, abide by rules, and consider the rights and needs of others.

—Sidonie Gruenberg
(1881–1974), Author, educator,
and director of the Child Study
Association of America

Do you know what amazes me more than anything else? The impotence of force to organize anything. There are only two powers in the world: the spirit and the sword; and in the long run the sword will always be conquered by the spirit.

—Napoleon Bonaparte
(1769–1821)

DISCIPLINING A SPIRITED child is as much about disciplining yourself as it is about disciplining the child. When a child misbehaves, it is the tendency of the parent to pick up the sword of discipline and attempt to scare the misbehavior out of that child. We threaten, we yell, we spank, we take away privileges, we time-out, we ground them into eternity—and yet, at the end of it all, we are still conquered by their spirit.

On one of my guest appearances on *The Montel Williams Show,* I spoke with two parents who were so defeated by their defiant four-year-old that they were willing to fly across the continent and air their personal failures on national television in order to get any advice that would help them. These were not weak and helpless people, either. In fact, the father was a SWAT team member! Yet short of child abuse, there was no way that his use of force could defeat his spirited son. The more the father fought, the more his son rebelled. The more the mother pleaded, the more her son rolled over her. It was clear that both needed to change their approach to discipline if they were ever going to tame this very spirited child. But change requires self-discipline, which is why I say that disciplining a spirited child is as much about disciplining yourself as a parent.

The problem begins in that most parents have been taught to use punishment to discipline a rebellious child. If a little punishment does not work, then we have been taught to use more and more punishment until the child eventually sees the error of his ways and knuckles under to our authority. This strategy sometimes works with the majority of children, and sometimes it backfires even with them. With spirited children, however, it almost never works. The more we punish, the more they resist. The more we bribe and cajole, the more they roll over us. They seem to have unlimited supplies of power to resist our attempts at control.

Clearly, we must do something different. Parents of spirited children need to learn to neither fight nor give in when their child misbehaves. Giving in only reinforces the child's mistaken belief that he should rule the roost. Fighting only reinforces the child's mistaken belief that he can control our emotions by making us angry and bringing us down to his level.

How to remain the leader in the family without fighting or giving in is the goal of this chapter. But in many ways, it is also the goal of the entire book, because discipline does not occur in a vacuum. It always occurs within the context of your relationship with your child. When the relationship is a positive one, then discipline flows smoothly as a necessary component of the entire parenting process.

But when the relationship is characterized by hostility, anger, and retaliation, discipline becomes a nightmare, with the child willing to submit to almost any punishment or indignity rather than give in to her perceived enemy. This is why so much of this book has to do with building the relationship between you and your child. The concept of taming is about building ties. The more positive ties we build with our children, the easier discipline becomes. So I caution you against jumping into this book at this chapter. Even though the discipline skills described here are respectful, and so designed to trigger the least amount of resistance in your spirited child, please read the entire book before beginning to use these skills. You will find that they work much better as you continue to use the relationship-building skills addressed in later chapters, as well as earlier ones.

What Is Discipline?

Let's clear up a misconception before we go any further. The word *discipline* does not mean "to hurt a child." Historically, we have acted as if the "no pain, no gain" philosophy of physical fitness applied to teaching kids right from wrong, good manners, family values, and positive behavior. We acted as if we had to hurt them either physically, emotionally, or by rescinding some privilege in order to teach them these concepts. Ironically, at one time we thought the same thing was true for teaching them reading, writing, and arithmetic, and there were scores of children with sore knuckles and reddened backsides who paid the price. Eventually educators found that kids actually learned better without the fear of punishment added to the equation, and today parents would be outraged if they heard of a teacher whacking a child across the knuckles for missing a math problem. Yet these same parents often still believe in the no pain, no gain principle when it comes to teaching behavior and values.

I have intentionally used the word *teaching* several times in this section, because the word *discipline* actually comes from the Latin word *diciplina,* which means "to teach." Discipline is how we teach children—whether math, English, science, and the other academic disciplines, or how to live within the rules and needs of the family and society. I might define it as a method of teaching children how to behave in socially useful ways by setting limits and enforcing them.

It does not mean "to hurt." Hurting children in order to teach them anything did work reasonably well for much of human history. As long as men were governed by superiors—in the form of kings, queens, emperors, czars, nobles, and other bearers of absolute authority—punishment and its twin sister, reward, kept people pretty much in line. But as the world progressed from these hierarchical societies in which people "knew their place," "spoke only when spoken to," and otherwise cowered before authority to our more democratic modern societies, reward and punishment became less and less effective.

Now, when you reward your child for behaving well, he no longer takes the reward as if he were a grateful peasant at the hands of a lord. In a democratic society, a reward becomes a sort of unspoken agreement. "I did something you liked, so you rewarded me. Therefore, in the future when I do that same thing again, I expect you to reward me again." Kids raised on rewards, bribes, and even praise do not develop the cooperative attitude necessary for true success in a democratic society. Instead they develop a "what's in it for me?" mentality coupled with a sense of entitlement that eventually drives parents, teachers, and others to dismiss them as spoiled brats.

When Tonya's parents offered her money to make her bed in the morning, she gladly accepted. This worked out reasonably well for her parents, who had little success getting Tonya to do any chore. In fact, it worked so well that they offered her money to load the dishwasher after dinner. Again, Tonya, being a reasonably bright child who appreciated the value of a buck, quickly agreed. All rocked along pretty well until one evening when the doorbell rang. Mother had her hands full, and Dad was reading the paper, so they asked Tonya to go see who was at the door. "OK," replied Tonya, "but how much will you pay me?" Mom and Dad looked at each other in disbelief, wondering what kind of money-grubbing monster they were creating.

In today's modern world, when you punish a child for behaving poorly, he no longer accepts his punishment as a recalcitrant peasant who deserves his fate. In a democratic society, when you hurt someone, you give that person the perceived right to hurt you back. Most adults have learned to allow the justice system to do our "hurting back" for us, as giving in to the urge to retaliate directly leads to more and more hurt for all parties involved. But children, and especially spirited children, are not as sophisticated in their application of justice. They just want to strike back, and they do, often with more force and hostility than the parent expects.

April's parents decided that it was time for their daughter to begin doing chores around the house. They told her that she would have to make her bed in the morning or there would be no TV that night. When April tested their new dictate by "forgetting" to make her bed, Mom was ready for her when she got home from school. "April!" she commanded, "march right into your room and tell me what is wrong with this picture!"

April did as she was told and, seeing the unmade bed, replied, "Oh, I guess I forgot to make it this morning."

"Well, then you understand why there is no TV tonight, don't you?"

"Mom, it's not that big a deal. I'll make it now."

"You're right, you'll make it now, but that doesn't change the fact that there is still no TV tonight."

"That's not fair! I said I'd make it, and I will."

"Yes, but I said you had to make it before you left in the morning, or there would be no TV that night, and I mean what I say. So there is no TV tonight. Now, make your bed and don't forget to make it tomorrow."

"No."

"What did you say?" replied an indignant mother.

"I said no. What's the point of making it now if I don't get to watch TV tonight anyway?" reasoned her spirited daughter.

"Because I said so!" boomed her mother.

"You want it made so bad, then you can make it yourself!" hollered April just as loudly as she stormed out of the room.

"You are grounded for a week!" her mother yelled after her.

"I hate you!" screamed April as she slammed the door and ran outside.

You may be thinking that what April needs right now is a good spanking. After all, she is being a mouthy, disrespectful child who needs to be taught a good lesson. This is what parents have been taught to think for centuries, and for centuries, as I've already pointed out, it worked pretty well. But today, especially with spirited children, this type of escalating punishment becomes a game of high-stakes poker, with kids upping the ante until nobody wins. The punishment trap is such that even if the child eventually gives in, she resents her treatment so vehemently that she looks for ways to get even later on. Since she knows our values, wants, and hot buttons like the back of a cereal box, finding ways to get revenge is pretty easy. And if all else fails, because we want so much to see them succeed in life, kids can always get even by playing their ultimate trump card: They can fail. They can fail at school. They can fail with friends. They can fail with tobacco, alcohol, and other drugs. They can fail with sex. They can even fail with the law. And in each case, the result is a heartsick parent who wonders where it all went wrong.

I'm not suggesting that every failed life is the responsibility of the parent. Some very good parents have had kids who have made some terrible choices for reasons no one really understands. What I am suggesting is that playing a game of reward and punishment just does not work very well with spirited children. We have to develop discipline methods that are more respectful while still teaching our children how to live within the limits of the situation and play by the rules. We can't afford to fight or give in. We have to remain strong but kind. We can tame our curious, adventurous, powerful, persistent, and sensitive (CAPPS) kids, but we have to be smarter about it than ever before. Just using an old carrot and stick will not cut it anymore.

First, Build the Corral

You tame a spirited child in the same place that you tame a spirited horse: a corral. No, not a literal corral, but just as a corral provides a structure for a wrangler to work with a wild horse, you have to build structures for your child in order to contain his wild energy and enthusiasm for life. Without such a structure, the call of the wild is just too great, and the horse bounds through the open range with a spirit as free as the wind.

There are three types of structures that you will need to build for your child:

1. Time corrals
2. Space corrals
3. Behavior corrals

A Brief Parable

A psychologist was walking on the beach one day when he came upon a young child sitting on the sand, watching the mighty ocean.

"What are you doing?" asked the psychologist.

"I'm watching the waves roll in," replied the child.

"What have you learned?" asked the psychologist, always looking to add a little meaning to a young life.

"That I can't stop the waves from rolling in," replied the astute child.

"And how does that make you feel?" asked the psychologist, because after all, he was a psychologist.

"Relieved," replied the child.

Time Corrals

Most kids want to do what they want to do when they want to do it. They do not like to be told when to do things or when to stop doing things. Spirited kids have the power and the persistence (P^2) to take this desire to a new level. The sooner that you can begin teaching your child that there is order to his universe, the better he will learn to accept that certain things need to happen whether he likes it or not. This lesson is a fundamental aspect of discipline: learning to accept the things we cannot change. It is also a cornerstone of good mental health, spirituality, and getting along well with others.

Kids may resist this learning. But just as the child on the beach was relieved to find that he wasn't in control of everything, spirited kids are ultimately relieved to discover that there is a power greater than themselves, not only at work in the universe but also at work in their own home. When parents or other adults do not step up to this challenge, their spirited children not only fail to learn good time management, they become anxious and discouraged about life in general. As it is a relief for children to know that they cannot stop the waves from rolling in, it is stressful for them to think they can.

Building time corrals for children teaches them that the world is not chaotic but orderly. We get up at a certain time, and we go to bed at a certain time. In between, there are other structured activities along with free time without structure. This combination of structure and freedom gives them a good sense of balance in the world and helps them learn to accept other "impositions." The earlier in their lives that you can establish the discipline of time management, the easier it will be. But even with older kids, it still can and needs to be done.

Why not let them just go with the flow, follow their own rhythms, and otherwise march to the beat of a different drummer, to use popular, if overused, expressions that all mean the same thing: let them fall asleep in front of the TV if they want to. For one thing, there are too many adults who sacrifice all sorts of success because they never learned to manage their own time. These otherwise talented adults oversleep regularly, fail to get their paperwork in on time, miss meetings, and find too many things falling through the cracks. The result is frustrated relationships with friends, significant others, and at work. Some find it impossible to even hold down a regular job, their self-discipline is so poor. For another thing, kids who learn to accept order in one area of their lives find it easier to accept order in other areas, too. Establishing time structures is a good first step on the road to self-discipline.

Step One: Buy a Timer

A kitchen timer should be standard issue for all parents, especially those with spirited children. In fact, they should send you home from the hospital with one tucked in between the diapers and the formula. I seriously caution you not to try anything in this chapter until you get a timer. And the younger your child is, the more important it is to have one. Young children have no real concept of an abstract concept like time, but they can understand that when the bell goes off, it's time to move on. Kids who can tell time may understand the concept of time, but they often have trouble telling how fast it passes. Watching the timer tick down will help them learn to estimate time increments on their own, so that eventually they will not need a timer. Plus, for all who procrastinate—and that includes all of us to one degree or another—a timer tells us that it's time "to get around to it."

Bedtime Routines

Let's start at the beginning of the day: bedtime. While we usually think of bedtime as the end of the day, I believe that what happens at bedtime actually sets the tone for the coming day and is therefore the first and most important aspect of a child's day. As someone once wrote, "Most of the world's conflicts are caused by too little sleep." A child who constantly goes to bed too late, often after hours of conflict and overstimulation, is likely to be irritable the next day. But a child who is gently "put down" by a loving parent, tucked safe and sound in a warm bed, is set for both a good night's rest and a great start to the next calendar day.

This does not have to be as difficult as it may sound. Even when our spirited son, Ben, was at his most spirited, we never had trouble getting him in bed at night. The reason was that we built a corral—a time structure. The sequence went like this:

1. **We began with bath time at approximately the same time every night.** It is useful to have a set time during the evening to begin the bathroom routine. Parents who vary bedtime for their kids from night to night do not give their children a chance to get into a pattern or habit. This makes it tough on the child, which makes it tougher on the parent, who is often caught in the awkward position of trying to get the child into bed when the parent wants him to go to bed. The result is often a child who stays up to all hours and never learns the discipline of going to sleep at a reasonable hour.

I realize there will be nights when exceptions need to be made. This is not a problem as long as you have a regular routine and schedule that operates on most nights. Since people are creatures of habit, once you have established a bedtime habit, it becomes a no-brainer. Nobody has to think about it, they just do it.

Bath time is one area where parents of spirited kids get a break, because spirited kids seem to have a natural affinity for water. In fact, you may find that you have more trouble getting your child out of the bath than into it. If that is the case, set a timer next to the tub and let your child know how much time she will have to play in the water. When the time is up, it's time to move to step two. For kids who do not naturally love the water, you can make bath time much more enjoyable by adding some tub toys, music, and making it a little fun. Our young daughter used to giggle and giggle when we'd shampoo her hair and make one long strand stand up like Alfalfa's in *The Little Rascals*. We'd show her what she looked like in the mirror as we laughed and said, "Alfalfa!" It sounds corny, but to a three-year-old it was physical humor at its most brilliant.

News Bulletin: Kids Like Fun

We interrupt our regularly scheduled section on time structures with this important announcement: The more fun that you can add to a boring or undesirable task, the more cooperation you will likely get from your child. No, you don't have to be a professional entertainer and make everything in life fun and games. Simply look for simple ways to make ordinary tasks less ordinary by adding some humor, making it a game, or otherwise injecting a little action into the activity. This gives kids something to look forward to. And when kids have something to look forward to (devious grin), you have something to hold over their heads when they are slow to cooperate.

For example, the child who likes to take a bath but still isn't too wild about putting his dirty clothes in the hamper can be told, "When you have put your dirty clothes in the hamper, then it will be bath time." This provides a strong incentive for him to put the clothes away. Details at eleven (well, actually tactic 3 in chapter 5).

2. **After bath time comes teeth brushing.** This may not be the most fun thing a child ever undertook, but with a little creativity, you can even make teeth brushing a positive experience. "Can you open your mouth wide like a lion?" For older kids, an electric toothbrush, if you have the budget, is a great addition to the bathroom decor.

3. **Step three is to put on the pj's or whatever your child likes to sleep in.** If he resists what you want him to wear, this is a good time to offer a choice. Remember: freedom within limits. Be flexible within limits that are acceptable for the situation. What difference does it make if he would rather wear a T-shirt and underwear instead of those adorable pajamas your mother sent for his last birthday? This is an area where it is good to give a little ground rather than stand firm and provoke a fight.

4. **Next, we move into story time.** Reading to kids has all sorts of wonderful benefits. First, it's the best thing a parent can do to help a child do well in school. From age one (or even younger) up to middle school, we read each night to each of our children for about twenty minutes a night. While they were young, we made sure to have lots of picture books, and as they matured, we found books that were just a little advanced for them to read to themselves. Our son particularly liked the humorous poetry of Shel Silverstein and *The Adventures of Captain Underpants*. Later, like most of his generation, he became captivated by that

Potter kid at Hogwarts. As they got older, we found that reading aloud plays, poetry, and even a movie script (*Men in Black*, to mention a favorite of Ben's) was a lot of fun.

In addition to academic readiness, reading is also a great bonding time between parents and kids. You get to snuggle up together on their bed and lose yourselves in some wonderful story or other adventure. Take the time to talk about what you read and encourage your child's observations and opinions. This will help her learn to think critically, and it will help you establish those all-important ties with your child that are the heart of taming.

5. **Prayer or other spiritual words.** I know that not every family is religious or even spiritual. But if you are, this is a nice calming activity that helps spirited kids continue to relax as well as connect with their spiritual side. If you don't want to use a formal prayer, you can always create something yourself—maybe just words of thanks for all that you and your family are grateful for. In our family, we liked to say prayers after turning off the lights. This sort of signaled the end of the day, and our kids would routinely yawn as we began the prayers, not from boredom, but from being conditioned that sleep was sure to follow. That's how effective a regular routine can become.

6. **Your own special ritual.** This is a time to make up your own special good-night ritual. It might include a little back scratching or massage, a poem, or something interactive. For Ben, I would put my hand on his head and say, "From my head to your head"; then on his chest, "From my heart to your heart"; and then on his hand, "From my hands to your hands. Think, feel, do, I love you." Pretty soon he began saying it with me, so that we ended with "Think, feel, do, I love you." It's a good thing to go to sleep

knowing that you are loved. You are incredibly important to your child, whether you've had a good day or a bad day. Make sure they seldom go to sleep without hearing from you that you love them.

Now, here's the beauty of this time structure. By forming a chain of events that includes some very desirable activities, you have built in incentives that keep the entire chain moving along to its natural conclusion: sleep. If the child balks at any part of the chain—for example, putting on her pj's—you simply have to say, "Honey, you can either put on your pj's now, or we will have to go right to sleep."

In other words, if any part of the chain is broken, the child misses out on the entire chain, with the exception of her "I love you" as you turn off the light and kiss her cheek. Stay calm, loving, and firm as you enforce the consequences of her choice to go right to bed. We will talk more in the next chapter about the use of logical consequences as a discipline tool.

Other Time Structures

A few of the other time corrals that you will want to build with your child might include the following:

- **A morning routine.** Let's face it, some kids are hard to get going in the morning, just as some adults are. It seems that their internal clocks are just set differently. On the other hand, many spirited kids are just the opposite. Ben was such a morning person when he was a toddler that we had to explain to him that he needed to stay in his crib until "the sun is up." Unfortunately, he got the spelling wrong, and the next morning about five o'clock we heard him yelling from his crib, "Son's up! Son's up!" With such kids, make sure that they know to stay in their room, or crib, and play quietly until the alarm clock goes off. Put out some books or other appropriate toys the night before for them to play with the next morning and remind them to play quietly.

Once it is time to get up, establish your time chain. Try to be consistent about a wake-up time, just as you are with a bedtime, so that they can get into a pattern. For example:

- Wake up. My wife was great about making sure our kids woke up to a loving voice and smiling face.
- Wash up. You will need to supervise younger kids, as at bedtime.
- Get dressed. Be sure to lay out the clothes the night before for younger kids. Older kids can choose their own clothes, and some will still benefit from choosing the night before to avoid morning slowdowns.
- Eat breakfast. Don't skip breakfast; it teaches good eating habits. But you don't need a hearty "American" breakfast, either. Simple and nutritious is just fine.
- Get going. Either to school or, if the child stays home, into some activity.

Figure out how long each step in the chain needs to take, then assign wake-up times that allow enough time for an unexpected delay or two. Too many families start the day harassed, which is not what you want to do with a spirited child. Allow plenty of time, but keep it moving.

- **Daytime schedule.** Daytime schedules will vary from family to family, and sometimes from day to day. If both parents work outside the home, then child care or school becomes a priority. Make sure that you provide a good one. You will need a provider who is experienced with children and has the skills to discipline lovingly and the patience to follow through. I'll talk more about working with schools in chapter 11, but, again, a good school is important. If you have one in your area, that's great. If you do not, consider moving or finding a good independent school.

If you are home during the day with your child, find "anchors" to do regular activities. For example, you might establish an art time, where the two of you get out the paints, clay, or coloring books and go at it. Or perhaps your child goes at it at the kitchen table while you are doing your work nearby. This has the advantage of providing company for each of you (again, establishing ties), supervision for the child, and modeling for the child that grown-ups also have work to do. Other regularly scheduled activities might include reading time, lunch, naptime, and, Ok, a little video won't hurt. Just don't turn it into an all-afternoon event.

If you are homeschooling your child, be sure to create a regular structure that includes a daily start time, start and finish times for each subject, built-in breaks, and a finish time. Do not fall victim to Parkinson's Law ("Work expands to fill the time available for its completion") by acting as if you have all day for schoolwork. Make a schedule and keep to it.

If your child is in school, schedule time for the following when he comes home:

- **Snack time.** A healthy afternoon snack that won't interfere with dinner is a good pick-me-up for many kids after a hard day at school. Involve your child is choosing which snacks will be available—as always, within acceptable limits.

- **Unstructured play time.** Kids often need time to unwind after school or just "chill." Build in some time for outside play if they are not playing a sport at school or some quiet indoors activity if they are.

- **Homework time.** Some kids prefer to do their homework in the afternoon to get it out of the way, while others would rather play for a while and then do it after dinner. Either way is fine, as long there is a set time for the child to take care of this important business. Again, involve the child in the decision making. Ask questions like these:

> *"Let's talk about when you are going to do homework this year. Would you rather do it before dinner or afterward?"*
> *"How much time should we allow each night?"*
> *"What time do you want to begin each day?"*
> *"What room would you like to do your homework in?"*

The idea is to create a routine so that homework will become just another good habit for your child. Where in the house your child works is not very important. Some kids like the kitchen table, where there are other people around, while others prefer a desk in their room and a lot of privacy. Some like music, while others like quiet. This is fine, except that you should prohibit loud music or TV during homework. Both have been shown to interfere with studying. Reading on her bed is fine, but writing papers on the bed is not. Lying down is just not conducive to good penmanship. Of course, if your child uses a laptop computer for writing, then she may very well be able to write well on the bed or elsewhere. It is helpful for you to keep the house quiet during homework time. Even better, you can model the importance of learning by taking the time to read and learn something yourself while your child does his homework. What better encouragement for doing homework than for him to recognize that he is part of a family of learners?

- **Dinnertime.** The family dinner is still an important part of most homes. Even so, time pressures and overscheduling have combined to make many otherwise conscientious parents resort to fast food and separate meals for parents and children. Some families just put the food out on the stove and tell everyone to help himself whenever he can. It's enough to make Norman Rockwell turn over in his grave.

Spirited kids, like all children, derive many benefits from having meals together as a family. In fact, children who have dinner with their family two times a week or less are significantly more likely to engage in harmful behaviors such as alcohol/drug use. Of course, spirited children also have the CAPPS to turn any meal into an atrocity. Sensitive kids may rebel at the idea of the gravy from the mashed potatoes having the audacity to ooze over onto the string beans. Powerful kids may let you know that they do not want any broccoli tonight by tossing it on the floor. A persistent child may decide that she wants ice cream for dinner and cry through three courses until she gets it or gets sent from the table.

Rather than trying to make sure that your child eats this and that in order to get a healthy diet, focus on what he *doesn't* eat. As long as you serve nutritious food and limit the amount of sugar in his diet, he will pretty much balance himself out. You don't need to force-feed him greens. If you want to make sure that he does eat his greens, my wife came up with a great strategy for our son. First, find out which greens he likes, or at least which greens do not make him livid. In Ben's case, it was steamed broccoli. My wife would serve him a dish of steamed broccoli as an appetizer, when he was most hungry. He usually gobbled it up without a problem. If he chose not to eat his broccoli, there was no begging or threatening. We avoided a power struggle by telling him this:

"Ben, the broccoli is the healthy food. Dessert tastes great, but it isn't all that healthy. So, if you want dessert tonight, then you need to eat your broccoli. If not, no problem, you can skip them both tonight."

Sometimes he did choose to skip them both. But remember, as long as you don't put too much sugar in the fuel tank, your child's engine will run pretty smoothly. Dessert is not used as a reward, by the way. We aren't rewarding him for eating his vegetables by giving him sweets. It simply recognizes the natural fact of human nutrition—namely, sweets will interfere with the body's natural ability to regulate its own needs. So the rule is "When you have eaten your nutritious food, you may have a little of the sweet stuff."

Please also keep in mind that many spirited kids are picky eaters. Work with them to find the foods they do like and stick with them. If they do not want to taste the eggplant, do not create a power struggle just to drive home the old "Try a bite, you might like it" philosophy. Instead, teach them to say "No thank you" and then respect their words. Ben, by the way, has now eaten broccoli for over three thousand straight meals, which means he is an automatic shoo-in for the Spirited Kids Hall of Fame. Yes, this is an exaggeration, but what is not is the fact that he is a very healthy child with limited likes and unlimited dislikes.

If you cannot have regular family meals, have them as often as you can. Among other things they:

- reinforce the fact that you are a family;
- provide an opportunity for teaching table manners;
- provide an excellent opportunity to establish ties through conversation, laughter, and encouragement;
- are usually more nutritious than meals out;
- provide opportunities to teach responsibility and cooperation through chores such as setting the table and helping prepare the meal.

- **Weekends and holidays.** Kids love them, and parents cringe. Without the blocks of time anchored by school each week, weekends and holidays can seem like a long blast from a loud horn. Spirited kids, full of curiosity and looking for adventure, can easily wind up creating enough chaos to keep themselves entertained (or frustrated) and you just frustrated. The key is to create some time structures to anchor those long periods of time. In other words, plan the days around some concrete activities that have specific times. This gives your kids something to look forward to. Whether it's reading time or a trip to the zoo, these events help create order and positive expectations in your child. Plus, it gives you some solid help when they begin to get restless. "You need to find something to play with for about thirty minutes, Jeffrey, and then we'll get ready to leave for the zoo. How about your blocks?"

Space Corrals

This sounds like something built by NASA cowboys, but in reality I'm talking about spaces a lot closer to home. Well, actually, I'm talking about spaces in and near the home. Structured spaces give your child a sense of security, as they provide limits to his movements and freedom to move within those limits. Let's look at a few of the most likely corrals in this area:

- **Your child's room.** Your child's room is her personal space—within limits. This means that you should allow her the freedom to choose how she would like to arrange the furniture, decorate the walls, and otherwise make it her own within limits that are acceptable to you. And by "acceptable," I don't mean that she has to make the choices that you would make. As long as she is not violating any health or safety standards, your budget, or family values, then help her make it a place where she is comfortable. Having her own space—even a part of the room if she shares it with a sister—helps show her that although she is part of a family, she is still an individual whose likes and dislikes are taken seriously. You can make suggestions, but do not force them. By all means, take her shopping with you when it's time to pick out things like drapes, bed coverings, and decorations for the room. Making it a cooperative venture can help build the relationship between the two of you as you show your caring and concern.

- **A quiet place.** Spirited kids need a place to calm themselves when things start to go awry. Some may like to lie on their bed, but others prefer a quiet chair or even a nook with a blanket and some pillows. Talk with your child about establishing such a place and find one that works for all of you. Then, during times when you sense that he is losing his temper, you can gently suggest, "It seems to me that you could use a few minutes in your quiet place." This is not said as a punishment but in recognition that removing oneself from agitation is often the best strategy for keeping one's cool.

- **A study place.** I wrote earlier about different kids preferring to study in different places. Talk with your child about a quiet place where she can study. Then help her arrange that space with a good light, pens and pencils, a dictionary, a computer (if she is of the age to use one), and anything else that the two of you feel is needed. Make this a joint project, so she will feel ownership of this space. This will help motivate her to work here, and, after all, doing homework and studying for tests is still a key part of success in most schools. Don't feel that your kids have to be locked in to this space. Some may use the space for writing assignments but then move to their bed or a comfortable chair for reading. The key is to have a home base.

- **A place to play outdoors.** Spirited kids have a lot of energy and need a safe place to use it. Being curious and adventurous, they will also tend to stray if they do not have clear boundaries. Your play corral does not have to be an enclosed yard, although a fenced-in area does make a clear boundary. With young children, you will need to keep an eye on them anyway as a safety precaution when they are outside playing. With older kids, you need to be very clear and firm about where they are allowed to play. This will depend on their age and the safety of your neighborhood. If you live on a busy street, then obviously your child needs to be limited to the yard; perhaps even the backyard. If you live on a lazy cul-de-sac with lots of kids, then perhaps it's safe for him to play in the cul-de-sac. You have to make the decision based on safety, but whatever that decision is, be sure to communicate it clearly to your child, and then monitor to make sure he abides.

  In order to ensure that he understands the importance of staying within the limits you set, provide him with a choice: "You can either stay within this area, or you will have to play inside the house." If he leaves the area, the consequence is that he loses the privilege of playing outside for the next day. We call this a logical consequence, a discipline tool that I'll cover in detail in the next chapter.

- **A knowledge of what's off-limits.** Children have to learn what is off-limits inside the home as well as outside. With very young children, you cannot count on teaching them this and must use gates to prevent them from going into either dangerous areas or areas that have not been childproofed. Take the time to childproof all of the areas that are open to them by crawling around on the floor at their eye level and seeing what danger or mischief they might get into. Then take preventive action. For example, cover plugs with guards; remove small pieces that might choke them, like marbles; make sure that pots and pans are not within reach to pull over on top of them. There are plenty of books that can help you think through all of these areas.

As kids get older, it is still a good idea to put what is off-limits out of reach and out of sight. If you don't want your child exploring your stereo, put it high enough that he can't easily reach it. You still want to tell your child what is off-limits, but taking away some of the temptation is helpful. Remember, spirited kids are curious.

This brings up the critical area of gun ownership. Each year many spirited kids die from accidental shootings because they found a parent's gun, played with it, and it went off unexpectedly. I personally recommend that parents of spirited children not keep a gun in the house. The chance that your child will use it to end his own life is greater than the chance that you will use it to save his life. It is just not worth the risk. If you have rifles for hunting or sport, keep them in a locked cabinet. If you forget to lock it even one time, then do the safe thing and get rid of them all until your kids are grown, or at least find a place away from home to store them. That is a reasonable logical consequence for your own misbehavior.

Behavior Corrals

Most parents are what I call *reactive*. That is, they wait for their child to misbehave, then they react. Their reactions usually include anger, harsh demands, and punishment. The result is often open power struggles with their child and/or retaliatory misbehavior later on. I called my parenting education program *Active Parenting* to stress the importance of being *proactive* in teaching children positive behavior. Parents who take an active role in establishing clear expectations for behavior find that they are able to prevent many of the problems that plague other families. Corralling behavior before it turns into misbehavior is a matter of establishing clear rules, and expectations for those situations in which your child's spirit is likely to lead him to run amok. When he knows the limits and is free to make choices within those limits, not only is he much more likely to behave well, but he also feels more secure about himself and his role in the family. If you think that it is strange to feel secure when one is restricted in such a way, consider the sad story of one man who didn't.

In the late 1970s when the Supreme Court had reinstated the use of the death penalty for capital crimes, a man was sentenced to the electric chair for murder. An interesting aspect of his execution was that he eschewed all efforts on his behalf to prolong his life. When he was asked by a reporter why he chose to die, he gave the following answer: "Because I grew up in a family where nobody ever told me what I could and couldn't do, and for me life has been a living hell." When the same reporter interviewed his mother, her statement was that "he was a good boy and just needed another chance."

One somber truth of this story is that some spirited children do not turn out well. These kids become more and more untamed, progressing into conduct disorders and eventually becoming criminals until someone finally puts them in a corral (prison) where they cannot hurt anyone. Sometimes their very lives are forfeited in the process.

Another truth is that kids, in spite of their protests, do not really want to live in a family where no one tells them what they can and cannot do. This is not the paradise that kids might think. It is instead "a living hell" in which they are at a loss to distinguish between acceptable behavior and behavior that gets them into trouble. A final truth from this sad story is that we do our children no favors by over-protecting them from the consequences of their misbehavior. The mother who complained that her murdering son was still "a good boy" and needed only "another chance" was the same mother who probably ignored his misbehavior when the stakes were still small and failed to teach him that misbehavior has consequences.

Kids need a code of behavior to live by. Whether you call this code "rules," "guidelines," "family policy," or something else, the idea is the same: There are some things in our family that you can and cannot do. These limitations corral spirited behavior in a way that the child cannot do for himself. This calls for the parent to be calm, firm, fair, and even flexible. It requires an active leadership role. And with spirited kids, it often takes courage. The result is worth the effort. As your child learns to live within the rules of the family, she is also learning eventually to live within the rules of society. The following suggestions can help you develop these rules effectively. In the next chapter, I'll help you with some ideas for enforcing them.

- **Focus on the rule, not the child.** One of the advantages of living in a society of laws is that the laws are impersonal. They aren't made to limit you personally but to limit everyone equally, or at least everyone in a certain category. By keeping laws impersonal and equal, there is less personal resentment. In addition, people do not mind being limited as much when everyone else is limited also.

- **State rules in general terms** instead of saying "You have to . . ." or "You may not . . ." For example:

  - "Bedtime is at eight o'clock" rather than "You have to go to bed at eight o'clock."
  - "No running in the house" rather than "Don't run in the house."
  - "We don't hit in our family" rather than "Don't you hit me!"

- **Use the phrase "in our family" to state familywide rules.** Helping children learn that they are part of a family is an important ingredient in developing their courage and self-esteem. Without going into a lot of theory, it also helps them accept family rules. After all, if we are all in this together, it makes sense that we all live by certain rules. Of course, if you say, "In our family, we don't hit," then *you* have to refrain from hitting, or you lose your credibility. In the next chapter, I will cover some discipline skills that work a lot better than hitting anyway. Some other examples of the "in our family . . ." form of stating rules include:

- "In our family, we take a bath before going to bed."
- "In our family, we put our dirty clothes in the dirty-clothes hamper."
- "In our family, we treat each other with respect."

- **With younger children, keep rules simple and straightforward.** Until the age of five or six, kids do better being told the rules by parents. Keep it short and simple, and use a kind but firm tone of voice. This is not a time for a big discussion but rather a simple transfer of information. Of course, if you are married or live with a significant other, make sure that you two are on the same page before making a rule. For example, if one of you makes the rule "We put away our toys when we are finished playing with them," and the other routinely allows the child to leave the toys lying all over the floor, the child is apt to follow the unspoken rule "You may leave your toys wherever you like." When the parent who made the rule then reacts angrily—"Didn't I tell you that you had to pick up your toys?"—the child is going to be justifiably angry at the mixed messages he is receiving.

- **Involve older children in rule making.** By age seven, most children can be involved in making the rules that they will live by. This does not mean that you are turning over the limit setting to the children (akin to letting the inmates run the asylum), it means that you are allowing them to participate in the democratic process by exercising a certain freedom of speech. When people of any age feel empowered to influence the process, they are a lot less likely to rebel in order to take over the process. When they help make the rules through negotiation, they are more likely to obey the rules than when the rules are simply dictated. In addition, kids who are involved in such decisions learn the valuable process of limit setting and problem solving, which will serve them well in their careers and other areas of their lives. You are still the parent, and you have to feel comfortable with what is decided, or you'd better not agree. You do not have to agree to a ten-thirty bedtime if you feel that nine o'clock is more appropriate for your child's needs. However, you might offer something like this: "If you are in bed by nine, then I'll allow an extra half hour for you to read by yourself." Try some of these phrases on for size:

- "Let's meet to discuss some guidelines for our trip to the beach."
- "We need to talk about your bedtime for this school year."
- "Let's talk about how much screen time is OK for you to watch."

- **Live by rules yourself.** Countless politicians and leaders of industry have demonstrated that nobody is above the law and that when you break the law of the land, you pay the consequences. Most parents, on the other hand, do not act as if rules apply to them. It is as if the little kid they once were still believes that "when I'm grown up, I'll be able to do whatever I want, and nobody can tell me not to!" Their kids see them saying one thing to them and doing the opposite when it suits them. This makes it more difficult for the parents to have the credibility to enforce the rules they set. Certainly there are some rules that apply to children but not to adults. But you will be on a much firmer setting if you also have rules that apply equally to everyone in the family.

For example, you might have a rule that there will be an hour of quiet time in the house every evening for reading and study. During this time kids begin their homework while parents model being lifelong learners by reading something themselves.

- **Don't make too many rules.** Some parents go overboard with rule setting and come up with a new rule every day or two. This is not the book of Leviticus, where the ancient Hebrews had over six hundred rules for governing every aspect of life. You will find that if you use rules sparingly, you will have better results in enforcing them. Maybe the ancient Hebrews actually understood this also, when they came up with a list of "most important rules" to live by, also know as the Ten Commandments. Parents who are constantly "shooing flies" by fussing over every aspect of their child's behavior are inviting power struggles. Focus on what is really important to you and your child, then take a firm stand on these issues.

- **Have some "megarules."** In order to keep down the number of rules in your family, come up with some megarules that cover a lot of behaviors. For example, a rule that "We will treat each other with respect" can cover everything from hitting to name calling. When a child violates this rule—for example, by yelling at a sibling—you can simply ask, "Are you treating your sister with respect?" Other megarules might include:

  - No hurting others.
  - Work before play.
  - Parents are in charge.

- **Enforce the rules consistently.** Rules are effective only if you take the time to make sure they are followed and then enforce the consequences when they are not. As they say in business, "You don't get what you *expect*, you get what you *inspect*." Kids will test us to see if we really follow through with our rules or if we will forget them or otherwise ignore them. In the next chapter, I'll talk about how to handle broken rules, but for now keep in mind that you will have to inspect to see if your rules are being followed. For example, if you make a rule that your child is to make her bed before coming down to breakfast, you have to check to make sure she has remembered to do so. Otherwise, it will not be long before she reverts back to her old habits.

Chores and Allowances

A special type of behavioral structure has to do with giving children chores and allowances. Not only do these activities teach children such valuable lessons as responsibility, reliability, and the value of money, they reinforce the notion that in a family everyone shares in the work of the household and also in the family resources. This promotes a sense of belonging that is fundamental to your child's self-esteem and motivation to cooperate.

Children as young as three can be encouraged to help out in the kitchen and in other ways around the home. Offering lots of encouragement when they do can help them get a sense that pitching in is rewarding in itself. At about the age of six or seven, they are ready to take on regular chores. Hold a family meeting to discuss who will do what, being sure to include the parents. Talk about the jobs that need to be done, including some of the ones that only adults can do. This will help the kids appreciate what is being done for them, so that when they are asked to contribute, it seems fair. Use group discussion to decide who will do what chores for the month. Be sure to meet again in a month so that no one gets stuck taking out the garbage for life!

It is tempting to pay children to do chores, but I advise against this. We want them to learn that pitching in with the work is something that all family members do to help run the home. Allowances are also something they get as members of the family. If they want to earn extra money, it is fine to give them other jobs such as shining your shoes or washing the car. Many families also make a rule that if a person does not do his chore by a certain time, then anyone else may do it, and the person whose chore it is must pay that person a predetermined amount for doing it for him.

I suggest starting kids on allowances by age seven, making sure they know what the allowance is expected to cover. With younger children, this may only be spending money to use as they wish. But it also gives you some leverage to avoid being nickel-and-dimed every time they want something. All you have to say is, "That's what your allowance is for, honey." As children get older, increase the allowance as well as what expenses it is expected to cover. With our daughter in college, her allowance covers pretty much everything—except her astronomical tuition.

Advanced Discipline: Heading Them Off at the Pass

> . . . *Misinterpreted rigor and discipline, a daughter of indolence,*
> *almost permits one generation to take revenge on the next for the*
> *thrashing it received itself and for the mishandling it has suf-*
> *fered—by treating the next generation in a like manner.*
>
> —SOREN KIERKEGAARD
> (1813–1855), *Soren Kierke-*
> *gaard's Journals and Papers*
> (1967)

AS LONG AS there have been kids, kids have tested the limits imposed by their parents. I can imagine a cave father telling his cave son ten thousand years ago not to go out looking for honey on his own, only to find his son hours later covered in honey—and bee stings. Some things in life are just too tempting for spirited kids to resist on their own. That's where parents come in. Through active use of effective discipline skills, we seek to redirect their misguided behavior (aka misbehavior) toward more positive behavior. We see them going astray, and we head them off before they go out of bounds. Or we provide a lesson that teaches them not to go out of bounds again.

We are not trying to change their spirit, break their will, or otherwise alter their God-given personality. We are attempting only to teach them to use their spirit for useful purposes in order to succeed personally and to make a contribution to the welfare of the community. We want to affect their thinking and their behavior. If we do this, we will also affect how they feel, so that life is ultimately more satisfying. Of course, as Kierkegaard observed over 150 years ago, how we discipline spirited children can be for better or for worse. Which brings us to what discipline methods work best with spirited children.

Eight Good Reasons Not to Spank

It may seem strange to begin with what *not* to do, but since spanking is still a popular, though diminishing, form of discipline left over from the Middle Ages, it deserves special mention. During one of my appearances on *The Oprah Winfrey Show,* I was asked why I didn't believe that spanking was a useful parenting method. It should be noted that this show came on the heels of a national news story about a mother who was caught on videotape abusing her young daughter in the backseat of the family van. I told the audience that I thought spanking was a high-risk method of discipline. Sort of like driving without seat belts. You may get away with it, but why take the chance? With spirited children, it is not only risky, it is likely to backfire and cause more problems. To elaborate, here are eight good reasons not to spank:

1. **It is easy for an enraged parent to cross the line from spanking to abusing.** The mother who was caught on videotape is a good example of how easily this can happen. The adrenaline rush produced by venting one's frustrations and anger on a child can create a "high" that can become habit forming, if not addictive. It feels so good to let it out. Unfortunately, by the time the smoke clears (and the videotape is found) many parents have crossed the line from spanking to hitting, shaking, slapping, and other forms of child abuse. This is why even parent educators who advocate

spanking say to never spank while you are angry. Calm down first and then calmly approach your child later. Of course, once you have calmed down, you can usually think of better methods of handling the problem than spanking.

2. **Spanking usually leads to more misbehavior.** Spanking a normal child often works to end the immediate misbehavior. Kids will usually "stop it this instant!" However, they also resent the spanking and seek out conscious or subconscious ways to get even. This usually takes the form of more misbehavior later or even aggressive behavior against other kids. With spirited kids, you get these negative side effects, plus you often get immediate resistance to the spanking itself. Instead of giving in, spirited kids will often dig in their heels and continue to fight you, kicking, hitting, and screaming bloody murder.

3. **Spanking models aggressive behavior.** Kids who are spanked regularly learn to handle many problems by hitting or threatening to hit. Others find that their parents are too big to get even with, so they take it out on other kids. In either case, in this time of zero tolerance for violence, such kids wind up suspended or even expelled from school. We have to teach kids that violence is OK only as a measure of restrained self-defense and never as a way to "punish" others for misbehavior or to impose your will. Spirited kids are enough at risk for getting into trouble at school without adding this extra dose of violence.

4. **Spanking can damage your relationship with your child.** Even if you spank your child only one time in her life, she may remember it the rest of her life and never feel quite as safe around you again. When you spank, you create a climate of hurt and

revenge that undermines much of the good in the relationship. Since the core of taming a spirited child is to establish ties, spanking runs counter to this goal. Whenever you hurt a child, you break some of these ties. You may be able to overcome this, but why take the chance when there are better discipline methods available?

5. **Spanking is out of step with the times.** When I was growing up in the 1950s, 95 percent or more of parents spanked. And I certainly got my share. And I turned out OK—didn't I? The fact is that spanking actually worked a lot better in the fifties and sixties than it does now. As a parenting method that evolved in the hierarchical societies of medieval Europe, it requires a society based on status to be truly effective. In our democratic society, with no group willing to play the inferior peasant class, everyone demands to be treated respectfully, even when disciplined. That's why we don't tolerate police brutality, public lashings, or the stocks anymore. In such a society, it was only a matter of time before kids too would start rebelling against physical punishment such as spanking.

6. **Spanking often leaves the parent feeling guilty.** Most parents are aware that spanking is now a controversial parenting method. The number of parents who spank has dropped to about 50 percent to 60 percent in recent years. The American Pediatric Association has come out against spanking. But even before this, many parents sensed that something was not right about hurting a child "for his own good" and felt guilty afterward. Parents need to parent from confidence in their methods and not guilt, and they can't do so when they intuitively know that what they are doing is hurtful.

7. *If* **spanking worked, parenting would be easy.** When I ask groups of parents or professionals if they agree that parenting well is difficult, everyone raises their hands. We all know how difficult it is. That's why parent education is needed and why so many groups are sponsoring courses like *Active Parenting*. I took my family to the San Diego Zoo a while back and was watching the gorilla pen. A parent gorilla was eating when a young gorilla began annoying her. She simply took a massive arm and backhanded the misbehaving child across the compound. My point? It takes an IQ of about 60 to hit a child, even to spank a child. If it worked to teach positive behavior in humans, then parenting would be easy, not difficult, because we can all do it. There must be more to effective discipline in our complex society than there is in the primitive society of apes.

8. **There are many more effective methods of discipline.** The bottom line in all of this is that there are better ways to discipline spirited kids in our modern society—methods such as polite requests, "I" messages, firm reminders, logical consequences, active problem solving, and the new FLAC method. These methods not only solve behavior problems but also help build qualities of character such as responsibility, cooperation, courage, respect, and even self-esteem. Do they work? Not by themselves, but if you use them in conjunction with the relationship-building strategies presented in this book, you will find that they work in ways that spanking, shall we say, can only ape.

Better Discipline Skills

The following discipline skills are in tune with the kind of society in which we live and will bring about better results when used with the other methods presented in this book. On the other hand, if you started with this chapter and plan to end with it, forget it. These skills will probably backfire like all of the reward-and-punishment methods you have already tried, and you can go back to complaining about how "nothing works" with your child. This may bring you some comfort in confirming your suspicion that you and your child are truly so unique that no parenting expert, psychologist, or anyone else can help. However, this will not enable either you or your child to live a more satisfying or productive life. And, of course, what it probably really means is that you have not yet mustered the self-discipline to apply the less macho methods of relationship building covered in other chapters of this book. The simple truth is that discipline does not occur in a vacuum. It always occurs within the context of a relationship. Work on that relationship before you work on the discipline if you really want to see improvement.

Having issued that caveat, here are some discipline skills that can help you redirect your child's misbehavior and keep him within the corrals you have developed in chapter 6. They are listed in order of firmness and intrusiveness, from least to most. Applying discipline to misbehavior is not like the invasion of Iraq. We do not want a strategy of shock and awe. In fact, we want to do just the opposite. We want to use the very least amount of force necessary to bring about change.

The reason for this is two-fold. First, when you use excessive force with a spirited child, it triggers his own power cells, and he digs in with more resistance. Add to this the spirited child's ability to persist, and you can get a power struggle that lasts for hours. Second, when a child changes behavior out of fear, he learns nothing about the need for cooperative behavior. Instead he learns, "I'd better do what they say when they are around, or else I'll really get it! But when they aren't around, I'll do what I want to do." These kids eventually wind up in trouble with other authorities. Using limited force, however, leaves the child thinking something along these lines: "I guess this really is the best way for me to behave in this situation." These kids eventually wind up making good choices in life and learning the value of cooperating with others.

The bottom line is that you will do better using these skills in order. If one does not work in a situation, then move to the next, and so forth, until the problem is resolved and your child is again living within the limits. If none of these measures works, then review the other chapters to see what you may be missing. If all else fails, pay particular attention to chapter 11 and look for help from outside resources such as a mental health professional.

Natural Consequences

The first discipline skill is, paradoxically, to do nothing. There are many lessons in life that a child will learn for herself if the parent will just stay out of the way and let Mother Nature do the teaching. These natural consequences of the child's choice of behavior have the benefit of putting the responsibility for the results squarely on the child's shoulders. Over time, these lessons in responsibility can add up to a very positive character trait.

Unfortunately, it is often difficult for parents to stand by and let nature take its course. After all, it is our job to protect our children. We cannot very well allow them to learn not to play in the street by getting hit by a truck. Whenever the natural consequences might be too dangerous, the parent has to step in and prevent them from occurring. However, there are many situations in which the parent could easily let natural consequences do the teaching. Instead, fearing that the child might be too unhappy or cause a problem, the parent gives in and undermines the discipline process. Consider the powerful lesson learned by philosopher Bertrand Russell's son (*Education and the Good Life,* 1926):

My boy had been coaxed into eating by his nurse, and had grown more and more difficile. One day when we had him for his midday meal he refused to eat his pudding. So, we sent it out. After a while he demanded it back, but it turned out that the cook had eaten it. He was flabbergasted and never made such pretences with us again.

What would have happened if Russell had been overconcerned with his son's eating and had the cook make another pudding for him or bring some other substitute? The natural consequence of hunger would have been lost, and the boy would have continued to expect the world to revolve around his whims. Experiencing a little disappointment, displeasure, and discomfort from misbehavior provides the motivation to challenge one's own decisions and make better choices in the future. Kids robbed of that motivation will usually continue to make the same mistakes and misbehavior over and over again.

Consider the following examples of natural consequences and where you might use them to help you redirect misbehavior in your home:

- When Jenny left her favorite book outside and it got rained on, her mother was sympathetic but gently refused to buy her a new one.

- When Tyler refused to wear his mittens to go outside and play in the snow, his dad did not fight with him. Later, when Tyler's hands were cold, his father gently asked him if he would like to go back inside and get those mittens.

- When the waiter told Lisa not to touch her plate because it was hot, Lisa reached right over and touched it. She looked up with hurt and surprise, saying, "It's hot!"

Experience is a great teacher, but we cannot always allow it to teach. Three situations in which parents must intervene and not allow natural consequences to teach include:

1. When the consequence is too dangerous.
2. When the consequence does not affect the child. For example, what if Jenny had left her sister's book outside and it rained?
3. When the consequence occurs too far in the future. For example, the natural consequence of not doing well in school is reduced career options later on. But it occurs so far down the road that most kids will not make the connection and so will not learn from the eventual experience.

In any of these situations, it is up to the parent to step in and provide more direct discipline. This brings us to the next method: polite requests.

Polite Requests and Gentle Commands

This may not sound like discipline to you, because after all, there is no disappointment, displeasure, or discomfort. But once your child has come to learn that you will follow your words with action— action that will cause some disappointment, displeasure, or discomfort—the words alone will get results. So we always start with the words, and sometimes they do get the results by themselves. And when they do not get the results by themselves, we move on to firmer communication and then concrete actions. But we always use words, because we eventually want our words to produce change by themselves.

You will also notice that I used the modifiers *polite* and *gentle* to describe the tone of voice that I would like you to use. Far too many power struggles begin because the way a parent asks or commands a child is either impolite or downright aggressive. The child may not really mind doing what the parent wants at the time, but the desire to be treated respectfully is so great that he resists almost out of protest. To keep your requests and commands polite and gentle, check the following:

- Use a friendly tone of voice.
  THIS: "Honey, time for dinner. Please wash your hands."
  NOT THIS: "Dinner's ready! Wash your hands right now!"

- Do not bring up past misbehavior.
  THIS: "Please wash your hands for dinner."
  NOT THIS: "I don't want to have to call you a dozen times like I did last night."

- Focus on the rule, not the child.
  THIS: "It's time to wash your hands for dinner."
  NOT THIS: "You need to stop what you're doing and wash your hands."
  THIS: "It's time to get ready for your bath."
  NOT THIS: "You need to get in the bath now."
  THIS: "The rule is we put away one toy before taking out another."
  NOT THIS: "You have to pick up your toys now."

Firm Reminders

I realize that just asking politely and gently is not going to get results all of the time with your spirited child. To begin with, people are creatures of habit. If your child is in the habit of dropping his dirty clothes on the bedroom floor instead of in the dirty-clothes hamper, he may have every intention of honoring your polite request, but he will continue to forget until a new habit is established. This can take a while even for the best of them. Rather than treat him as a rebellious insurgent, think of him as a student who needs repetition in order to establish new neural connections in order to master a new concept. Just as a student needs drilling and practice to sometimes "get it," the same is true of your child's behavior. A firm reminder can help jog his memory as he works to establish this new habit.

Another reason that your child may not heed your polite requests is that he just does not want to. What he would rather do is eminently more rewarding than what you want him to do, so he just ignores your requests and does what he wants. Spirited kids, being powerful to begin with, often do what they want to do when they want to do it. This is further complicated if you have been in the habit of yelling at him to get him to do what you want. He may take your polite and gentle request as a sign that you are not really serious about his behavior, and that it is safe to ignore you until you start yelling as usual. Of course, many spirited kids will just take yelling as an invitation to rebel, and before you know it you are in a full-fledged power struggle. Changing his expectations by beginning with a polite request is the first step to changing the relationship from one of conflict to cooperation. Don't backslide into yelling if you are serious about taming him. Instead, use a firm tone of voice and remind him in as few words as possible about what you want and expect. For example:

"**David,** the clothes—in the hamper."
"**Latisha,** plates in the sink."
"**Carl,** finger out of nose."

After you have made a firm reminder, stand there until your child complies. You may have to repeat the reminder if she ignores you or protests. Stay firm but never hostile, and let her know that you mean what you say. If you make a firm reminder but walk off and forget about it for an hour, she learns to ignore you. So plant yourself like a tree and do not budge until your child does. If she flat-out refuses or continues to ignore you, move to the next tactic, "I" messages.

"I" Messages

I messages are four-part communications that are remarkably effective in breaking through predictable and ineffective parent-child conflicts of the "You will!" "I won't!" "You'd better!" "You can't make me!" variety. Most parents have no idea how predictable they are to their children. We nag, lecture, threaten, bribe, yell, ground, issue time-outs, hit, and/or give in with such predictability that our kids know what is coming long before it actually comes. So why do they continue to misbehave if the results are often so negative for them? The answer is that their spirited temperment is more compelling than our desire that they change their behavior. Their own CAPPS continue to urge them on in spite of our efforts to discipline. In addition, they may be getting another payoff from the misbehavior: the sense of power that comes from seeing someone so big and important in their world brought to the brink of tears in total frustration. After all, for a child to control our emotions is a very powerful thing from the child's point of view. "I may not get my way, but I can sure show them how powerful I am by refusing to let them have their way!" Remember from our discussion on power in chapter 5 that it is important to *do the unexpected* and *neither fight nor give in*. Polite requests and firm reminders begin this shift in expectations, and I messages follow the same path with a more complete response. Here is an example of an I message:

"Kathy, I have a problem with you not coming inside when I call you. I feel very frustrated having to run after you when it's time to come in, because dinner is cooking, and I don't want it to get burned.

From now on, I'd like you to come inside when I call you. Will you do that?"

At first blush, you may think that there is not a chance in heaven that Kathy will honor her mother's request and suddenly change her misbehaving ways. But you might be wrong. Parents have told me over the years that I messages worked surprisingly well for much misbehavior with many children. One mother came back to an *Active Parenting* group that I was leading and reported:

"You wouldn't believe what happened. Danny has a bad habit of jumping up from the table as soon as he has wolfed down his food, which takes all of about three minutes. Last night I was ready with an I message. As soon as he started to get up, I said, 'Danny, I have a problem with you leaving the table before the rest of us are finished with dinner. I feel disappointed because we miss out on your company. I would like you to sit back down and stay with us until dinner is over.' Well, his head turned toward me like it was on a swivel. It was like the first time he had ever really heard me. He sat back down, and we had an enjoyable meal. Seems kind of simple now."

Although this is a true story, I messages will not solve every problem with a spirited child, but, again, they do the unexpected, which helps to change the dynamic between parent and child. Let's take a look at the steps of an I message to see how they are constructed:

1. **State the problem: "I have a problem with . . ."** I messages get their name because they begin with the word *I*. This is fundamentally different than how parents usually begin a confrontation with a child; for example, "You always jump up from the table while we're still eating . . ." When we begin with the word *you*, we put the child on the defensive, and a conflict is likely to ensue. By owning the problem ourselves, we communicate a more "we're in this together" attitude that defuses some of the tension right off

the bat. It also clearly states the problem so that both parties know what issue needs to be resolved. This is a good problem-solving procedure that will serve the child well throughout his life.

2. **Share your feelings about the problem: "I feel . . ."** By keeping the focus on you and your feelings, you again reduce the risk of locking horns in a power struggle. At the same time, you are teaching your child how his behavior affects others. This lesson in empathy is particularly valuable with spirited kids, who are often so into their own wants and sensitivities that they are oblivious to the feelings of others. We will focus more on the importance of empathy training and feelings in chapter 11, but for now, learn to use a feeling word to describe one effect your child's misbehavior has on you. Be on guard, by the way, against using the word *angry* too often. When parents begin using I messages, they are often in power struggles with their child and *do* feel angry. However, the trick is to catch yourself before you get angry and to focus on other feelings. For example, it is much easier for a child to hear that you are disappointed, hurt, worried, concerned, or frustrated than angry. Again, this reduces his defensiveness and opens up the possibility of change.

3. **Share the reason for your feelings: "Because . . ."** When Kathy's mother shared that she felt frustrated having to chase after her daughter when she called her to come inside, she did not leave it at that. She gave Kathy a reason for her feelings: "because dinner is cooking, and I don't want it to get burned." People often need reasons to motivate them to change behavior. Just telling our kids the problem and how it makes us feel may not be enough. Adding that we have a good reason to feel as we do can often swing the balance of reason in our favor. Of course, if your spirited child is out of control at the time, none of this is going to work until you calm her down. We will cover

methods for doing that in chapter 10. But for times when your child's mind is engaged, stating your reasons is a useful step.

4. **Tell your child what you want: "I would like . . ."** Some parents skip this step. Others are all about this step and skip everything else. The first group tends to believe that if you tell your child how you feel about something, the child should just correct his misbehavior on his own. Spirited kids do not work this way. You have to let them know clearly what change in behavior you would like. Use a firm but non-aggressive tone of voice and make direct eye contact when you say this. Parents who use only this step, skipping the feeling steps, tend to believe that if you tell your child what you want him to do, he should just do it. Spirited kids do not work this way, either. They take commands as orders and orders as invitations to fight. The feeling steps help reframe this into something less challenging, while the "I would like" step gives clear guidance about what change is wanted.

5. **(Optional) Ask for agreement: "Will you do that?"** It is sometimes advisable to close the deal by asking for agreement. This is particularly useful when the change that you want to take place occurs in the future. Kathy's mom is less interested in Kathy coming in for dinner right now than she is about Kathy coming in for dinner when she calls her in the future. Asking for agreement will help your child remember what you want. It will not guarantee that she remembers, but it will help improve the odds.

6. **(Optional) Ask for a time commitment: "When?"** There are many cases when your child will agree to do what you want—for example, cleaning up his room—but not exactly on the schedule you had in mind. You may be thinking "sometime today," and he may

be thinking "when hell freezes over." Unless it is exceptionally cold outside today, there is likely to be a time gap in expectations. To close this gap (and reduce the likely conflict later when you say, "You said you'd clean your room!" and he says, "I will!"), finish your I message by asking when the behavior will take place. If he hedges and says something ambivalent like "later," pin him down by saying *"when* later?" Be gentle and flexible but also persistent until you get a time frame that you both can live with. Then follow up later to make sure it is done.

7. **(Important!) If he changes his behavior, be sure to express your appreciation.** The best way to keep a behavior change going is to follow it up with encouragement. "Thank you, I appreciate it; your room looks great!" "I appreciate your coming when I called." There are endless ways to encourage positive behavior, and we will focus on more of them in chapter 9. For now, please know that the best way for you to sabotage an I message or any other discipline method is to fail to acknowledge progress and change. If your child goes to the trouble to change in ways you have requested, and you ignore that change, she is likely to think, either consciously or subconsciously, one of the following counterproductive thoughts:

- "I got attention for doing what she didn't want. I got ignored for doing what she *did* want. I like attention more than being ignored. I'd better go back to doing what she doesn't want, so I can get noticed again."

- "I went to the trouble of changing, and he didn't even notice. I guess it didn't really matter to him that much anyway, so I'll just go back to doing what I prefer anyway."

- "There is an unwritten contract in our civilized society that when one human being does something to fulfill a request made by another human being, the second human being is obligated to respond with at least a thank you and perhaps even an outpouring of gratitude. When this contract is broken, the first party is free to take whatever revenge he deems necessary, including but not limited to revoking said behavior change."

Lawyer humor aside, it is very important to encourage any positive change that your child shows, particularly when you have asked for that change. So stay on your toes and catch 'em being good.

Logical Consequences

So far the discipline methods that we have been discussing are communication skills. They increase in intensity and are gradually more confrontational. Yet they all have one thing in common: They appeal to the child's desire to cooperate with his parents. This is why taming a spirited child depends so much on our ability to build ties and establish a positive relationship. Even so, there are times when a kid needs an added boost in order to overcome a bad habit that has served his needs in some way in the past. Mere cooperation may not be enough.

Old-school forms of discipline either require that you hurt your child in some way in order to break him of his bad habits (or his blatant rebelliousness) or that you bribe him in some way with charts, stars, and incentives. I've already explained the downside of each of these approaches and want to suggest a third option. Children, and especially spirited children, need to learn that behavior produces consequences. When they choose to ignore your reasonable requests, the family rules, and the needs of a situation, they do not simply get away with it. They must pay the logically connected consequence that you as the leader in the family choose to enforce. These logical consequences are respectful and humane, to be sure, but they are designed to bring about some degree of displeasure to the child.

Notice that I did not say some degree of *pain and suffering*. We do not want to use such severe consequences that the child learns that he is cooperating only to avoid disaster. When this happens, he learns to blame his changed behavior on his parents. ("They made me change, and I resent it!") We want just enough discomfort that he will rethink his misbehavior but still feel responsible for the outcome. "I am responsible for my changed behavior, and it is working out better for me." This produces an incredibly important character trait in the child: responsibility. When kids realize that their choices lead to logically connected consequences, they are empowered to make better choices in the future. This sense of personal responsibility enables them to learn from experience, a cornerstone of success in any society.

The key to using logical consequences is to find a consequence that can be logically connected to the misbehavior. Most old-school punishment is pretty arbitrary. A child speaks disrespectfully to his parent, and he is sent to his room. He refuses to eat his peas at supper, and he is sent to his room. He won't pick up his toys when he is finished playing with them, and, you guessed it, he is sent to his room. This "one size fits all" approach to discipline, though easy to use, does not make logical sense to the child and so does not teach responsibility. In fact, it also undermines cooperation and leads to more rebellious behavior later on.

Now, there is nothing wrong with sending a child to his room if that particular consequence is logically related to the misbehavior. For example, if a child speaks disrespectfully to a parent, it is logical that he be separated from the parent for a time. Sending him to his room until he can talk more respectfully might be a good logical consequence for such misbehavior (although it may be difficult to enforce, but we will talk about that later). However, what does being sent to one's room have to do with the other two examples: refusing to eat peas or not putting away toys? The answer is nothing. It is an arbitrary consequence, the goal of which is only to punish, not teach. The same can be said of spanking, grounding, no dessert, and any of the other popular punishments that have been used forever.

Children are much more likely to see consequences that are logically connected to the misbehavior as fair. They may not like the consequence, but they are not as likely to feel attacked as they are with punishments. So the first step in using logical consequences is to retrain yourself to think logically when it comes to discipline. Like most parents, you probably have one or two favorite punishments that you continue to use because they occasionally get some good short-term results. This has been easy for you, if ineffective. To change to logical consequences, you will have to work at coming up with consequences that are truly connected to the misbehavior. For example:

- When Todd won't eat his vegetables, he has to leave the table and miss out on dessert.

- When Jennifer refuses to pick up her toys after playing with them, Mother puts them in a box, and she cannot have them for a day.

- When ten-year-old Todd gets angry and calls his father "dumb" because his father won't let him watch a PG-13 movie, his dad calmly leaves the room. After Todd calms down, his father explains to him the importance of speaking respectfully to people, especially his parents, and gives him the logical consequence of no movies or TV for the rest of the week.

Each of these consequences is logically connected to the misbehavior. But there is more to using logical consequences than just logic. Keep the following tips in mind, and you will have a much greater chance at success:

Keep Your Tone and Manner Firm and Calm

One key to effective discipline is to come across to your child as a strong, in-charge parent who is also on her side. Your voice, facial expression, and body language should all express this attitude of benevolent leader. Not dictator, but leader. You will lead, and it is up to the child to follow that lead. It is your job, your responsibility, and you have the skills to do it well. Your calmness reinforces your power. When parents get angry and even enraged, they look to the child as either an enemy or an inept dictator. This triggers in spirited children a desire to rebel. These rebellions take the form of ongoing power struggles in which nobody wins. On the other hand, when a parent sounds and looks weak to a child, ironically, that parent sends the same message of ineptitude. Spirited kids will take advantage and walk all over such parents. Firm and calm sends the message "You may not get what you want, but you are safe, and I'm here to help you grow up into a successful, contributing, and happy young person."

Ask Your Child to Help Solve the Problem

Dictators give orders and mete out rewards and punishments to children. Doormats plead and beg children to do their bidding. A more respectful approach to parenting is to treat the child as a thinking individual capable of helping to solve the problems she's created. With this is in mind, ask your child for help in coming up with logical consequences, not as a punishment, but to help her remember what habit is to be changed. For example, in the case where Kathy would not come to dinner when called, her mother used the following I message:

"Kathy, I have a problem with you not coming inside when I call you. I feel very frustrated having to run after you when it's time to come in, because dinner is cooking, and I don't want it to get burned. From now on I'd like you to come inside when I call you. Will you do that?"

If Kathy agrees to come in but then forgets or refuses to come in when next called, her mother might say the following:

MOTHER: "Kathy, we still have a problem with your coming inside for dinner when I call you. What do you think we can do to help you remember?"

KATHY: "I don't know."

MOTHER: "I was thinking that you might need a logical consequence to help remind you to come in when I call. How about this: Either you can come in when I call you, or your food will get cold, and it won't taste as good? Do you think that might help?"

KATHY: "I don't know."

MOTHER: "Me neither, but let's try it and see."

Sometimes kids will be much more creative than young Kathy appears to be in this example, but in any case, you will want to have a logical consequence in mind in case their involvement is just as minimal. By the way, it is not as important that they contribute substantially as it is that you offer to involve them. The simple act of involving them in the process helps head off the desire to rebel and can win cooperation later.

Give "Either-or" Choices or "When-Then" Choices, but Give a Choice
As presented in chapter 5, choice is power. Give your child a choice rather than an order, and you give him legitimate power. This, again, lessens the desire to rebel against your authority as a way of gaining (illegitimate) power. There are two basic forms for giving choices:

Either-or choices. *"Either [do what the situation or rule calls for] or [experience the logical consequences that I will set up to help you learn]."*
For example:

- "Either come inside when I call, or your food will get cold."
- "Either come inside when I call, or you won't be allowed to play outside before dinner the next night."
- "Either come inside when I call, or I'll have to put what you are playing with away for a day."

One of the wonderful things about logical consequences is that there are as many of them as you and your family's imagination can think of. In fact, in *Active Parenting* groups, parents brainstorm and share ideas about logical consequences that have worked in the past or might work in the future.

In every case, though, it is up to the parent with the problem to choose a consequence that he or she is comfortable with. Never give a child a choice with which you are not OK. In one class, a parent said that she would give her child the choice of either putting her dirty dishes in the dishwasher or leaving them to pile up in the sink until she did. The leader astutely asked this mother if she would be OK with dirty dishes piling up in the sink. The mother laughed and replied that, no, they would drive her crazy. This mother needed to find a different logical consequence—one that she could live with!

When-Then choices. "When [you have done what you don't want to do], then [you may do what you do want to do]." For example:

- "When you have put away your toys, then we will read your story."
- "When you have had your bath, then you may watch a little TV."
- "When you calm down, then we can talk about what you want."

The logical consequence in a when-then choice is a little more implicit than with an either-or choice. The unspoken message is that if you choose not to do what is required, then you do not get to do what you want. It is a sort of work-before-play philosophy. Be sure that you understand that this is not a bribe or even a reward for positive behavior. It simply takes two activities that happen anyway—like putting away toys and reading a story—and orders them so that the less-desired activity must be completed first, or the more-desired activity does not occur. A reward, on the other hand, offers the child something extra for doing what we want him to do. As I've explained before, this teaches the child a "What's in it for me?" attitude that undermines cooperation in the long run. When-then choices keep it real and are incredibly effective at motivating kids to do things they would rather not do or have not developed the habit of doing yet.

Give the Choice One Time, Then Act Consistently

Parents are always saying that their children do not listen to them. This is inaccurate. Kids do listen to their parents. They listen, and if their parents tell them to do something they do not want to do, they ignore them. Ignoring is not the same thing as not listening. The reason kids ignore us is that we often forget to follow through with the consequences of what we say. For logical consequences to be effective in getting your child to respond to your words, you have to follow up those words with action. If you give your child a choice, and she ignores you or out-and-out refuses, then you must firmly and calmly enforce the consequences. This communicates that you mean what you say. When she understands that you mean what you say, she will begin responding to your words alone, just assuming that the consequences will follow. Then you will have a child who does listen to you.

Another reason to give the choice only one time and then act is so that you will not get angry. The more you repeat yourself, and the more she ignores you, the angrier you get. We will discuss anger more in chapter 10, but for now, work to act *before* you get angry. Also, resist the temptation to lecture about how she brought this on herself and how she has to learn to do what you ask, blah, blah, blah. This will just make her want to ignore you even more as a way to get even for your insulting lecture. Instead, stay as friendly as possible and let the logical consequences do the teaching. For example:

- EARLIER: "Either come inside when I call, or your food will get cold."
  LATER: "I'm sorry, honey, but your dinner got cold while you were outside playing."
- EARLIER: "Either come inside when I call, or you won't be allowed to play outside before dinner tomorrow night."
  Later: "You didn't come inside when I called you for dinner. So remember that you will have to play inside tomorrow."
- EARLIER: "Either come inside when I call, or I'll have to put what you are playing with away for a day."
  Later: "Because you didn't come in when I called, we are going to have to put away those skates for a day to help you remember. Now, come in and wash your hands for dinner, sweetie."

I know the thought of sounding pleasant ("sweetie?") when disciplining sounds foreign, but remember that your goal is to neither fight nor give in. The consequence says that you have not given in, and the pleasant (or at least calm) tone of voice says that you will not fight. Because kids will test to see if we are really going to follow through with the consequence without fighting or giving in, expect the problem to persist for a while. But if you check to make sure that they have complied with the expectations and follow through consistently with the consequences, they will usually give up testing and change behaviors. After all, kids don't do what doesn't work. Without a payoff of you giving in or fighting, the logical consequence is not worth it.

Obviously, not every logical consequence matters to every child. I used three examples of logical consequences for the problem of not coming in for dinner when called. It may be that only one of these will work with your child. It may be that *none* of them will work, and you will have to think of another consequence to try. You are in the best position to know what will motivate your child. But whatever you decide, make sure that you can live with the results for a while as your child tests you. Then, if you see that the consequence just does not matter to your child, look for a new one to try the next time.

Of course, if you use the FLAC method described in the next chapter, and the other skills presented in this book, you may not need logical consequences at all.

FLAC: The Ultimate Discipline Tool

The greatest blessing of our democracy is freedom. But in the last analysis, our only freedom is the freedom to discipline ourselves.

—BERNARD BARUCH (1870–
1965), American financier,
statesman, and presidential
advisor

SPIRITED CHILDREN NEED discipline in order to be tamed, but where does that discipline come from? In the preceding two chapters, I've made the case for parents setting good structures and limits for their children (corrals) and then using respectful forms of discipline to enforce these structures. I have stressed that discipline that is either too heavy-handed (autocratic, dictatorial styles) or too lenient (permissive, doormat styles) is likely to exacerbate the child's natural tendency toward wildness and a lack of respect for others. Spirited kids who are treated in these ways often wind up in prison, on drugs, or otherwise at odds with their society.

But although spirited kids need a firm hand from parents and other authority figures in their lives, the goal of discipline in a democracy is not blind obedience to authority. As the Baruch quote suggests, our goal as parents is to teach our children *self*-discipline. We cannot do that without a certain amount of negotiation in the discipline process. Just laying down rules and enforcing them with logical consequences may corral a child, but by itself it will not teach him the essential lesson of self-discipline. In addition, when parents attempt to discipline only using consequences and the other methods presented in chapter 7, they run the risk of pushing too hard and escalating conflicts into power struggles. Something more is needed.

I have been teaching logical consequences and these other methods to parents for over thirty years, and they are very effective for most children—even with many spirited children. But when I stopped to look at what I was doing with my own kids—even my spirited child, Ben—I was surprised by how little I actually had to use these methods. What I noticed was that I had been doing a number of things first that often undercut the need to use logical consequences at all. As *discipline* means "to teach," I had been teaching my children how to stay within the limits without relying heavily on consequences. These tactics can be broken down into the four steps of the FLAC method, which I immodestly refer to as "the ultimate discipline tool." It is not "ultimate" because it scares children into submission or has some magic involved, but because it shifts the discipline from the parent to the parent and child in cooperation. When kids are involved in the process of finding solutions to problems, when their thoughts and feelings are taken into account, when they are regarded as active agents in their own lives, they are much more inclined to cooperate.

The four letters of the FLAC process, an acronym meant to reduce the amount of *flak* in your relationship with your child, stand for: Feelings, Limits, Alternatives, and Consequences. Let's take an example of a situation in which a parent uses the FLAC method to help tame her spirited son who is hypersensitive about what shirt he wears in the morning. As you read the account, see if you can identify where his mother uses the four steps of feelings, limits, alternatives, and consequences.

Five-year-old Adam sat on his bed in a huff, refusing to put on the yellow T-shirt his mother had laid out for him. "No!" he said with authority.

"What's wrong?" asked his mother. "I thought you liked yellow."

"I hate it!" said Adam.

"I see," said his mother in a calm and thoughtful voice. "You feel very strongly about this shirt."

Adam nodded, his lips held tightly together in defiance.

"Well, I don't want you to wear something you hate. But we have to get going so you can get to school on time, and I can get to work. Got any ideas?"

"Can I wear this?" asked Adam, pointing to the pajama top he was still wearing.

Mother laughed a friendly laugh and said, "That top feels nice and soft, doesn't it? I can see why you'd like to wear it. It would be pretty funny, too, you showing up in your pajamas while everyone else had on school clothes. Your teacher might just put you to bed. Now, maybe if they had a pajama day, and everyone wore pj's on the same day, that would be cool."

"Yeah, can we?" asked Adam, perking up.

"I can't promise, but I'll suggest it to your teacher if you'd like. But in the meantime, what are we going to do about today? How about wearing this red shirt?"

"No! I hate it, too."

"Wow, we are running out of options, and if we don't get downstairs in five minutes, we'll miss breakfast and have to eat something quick in the car. So let me ask you, which of the shirts in your drawer do you hate least?"

"The green one, I guess."

"Then the green one it is!" said Mom cheerfully as she put it down in front of her son. "You get dressed in a hurry, and I'll go down and get breakfast ready. And by the way, what do you want today, oatmeal or cornflakes?"

I realize that such conflicts do not always work out as well in real life as they do in a scripted dialogue. Sometimes spirited kids are too emotionally flooded to respond to the FLAC method, or anything else, until they have calmed down. We will talk about some of these self-soothing methods in chapter 9, but in many cases FLAC works wonders to establish ties with your child while teaching him to solve problems. Let's look a little more closely at how Mother used the four steps of FLAC with Adam.

Feelings

The first letter of FLAC, *F*, stands for "feelings." This is short for "acknowledge and accept your child's feelings, including what he wants and doesn't want." Nobody likes to be told no, and spirited children, with their propensity for power, like it less than most. But even more than being told that they cannot have what they desire, people like it even less to be told no by someone who does not seem to even care about what they want or how they feel. These "hard" no's come across as in-your-face rejections that trigger the desire to rebel rather than accept the authority's dictum. If Mother had said, "I don't have time for this, Adam. Put on this shirt right now, and I don't want to hear another word about it!" she probably would have triggered an emotional outburst that could have lasted hours.

Instead, she acknowledged her son's feelings by asking what was wrong. When he replied that he hated the shirt, she did not belittle his feelings by saying "You don't really hate it, Adam," or "This is a perfectly good shirt, please put it on." Instead, she simply let him know that it is OK to have his feelings, by saying, "You feel really strongly about this shirt." She also could have said, "Boy, you hate this shirt so much, you wish that somebody would just make it disappear, I bet!" The point is that whatever the child feels or wishes for is OK. And when he knows that we accept his feelings, then he can trust us enough to relax his guard.

In the opening example, Mother makes this transition from empathy/fantasy to reality by joining her son in his wish to wear pj's to school. She even goes so far as to say that she will ask Adam's teacher about possibly holding a pajama day for class. But then she nudges him back to the reality of the moment by asking, "What are we going to do about today?" This lets him know that pj's are outside the limits for today, and that they still have a mutual problem to solve. The fact that they are now in it together helps reduce the likelihood of a power struggle, while building a cooperative approach for finding a solution. It is important to keep your tone of voice firm yet friendly during this step in order to communicate this esprit de corps. If you suddenly turn demanding and aggressive, the empathy from step one will be revealed as a sham. You really have to feel that you are in this together and that solving the problem in a win-win fashion is what you really want.

When you acknowledge the legitimacy of someone's feelings, you gain an ally. It is as if the other person's subconscious mind says, "Hey! She understands me. She gets how much I detest this shirt, and she isn't mad about it. Maybe I can work with this lady."

Humans are incredibly social beings. For centuries we have thrown our lot in with one another as a way to survive and thrive on a hostile planet. Despite our protestations, we do care about what others think about us, because their thinking will often dictate how they will treat us. Our children are particularly sensitive to how we think and feel about them. They want our acceptance and our unconditional regard. True, they also want their way, even in situations where we cannot give it to them. But the trick is to set and enforce limits in such a way that we let them know that we still love and accept them as people—special people whom we value above all else. Listening for the feelings that lie beneath their words is one way that we can transcend the natural barrier between having to say no and maintaining a positive relationship. Consider these examples between giving a hard no and a feeling response, and how you would respond if you were a spirited child:

HARD NO	FEELING RESPONSE
"Get in bed this instant."	"It's hard to go to bed when you're not feeling very sleepy."
"No, you may not have another cookie."	"Those cookies are really good, aren't they? I wish I could eat a dozen of them!"
"I want you out of that tub right now."	"You really enjoy your bath time, don't you?"
"Stop crying and pull yourself together."	"You are really frustrated right now. It feels like everything is out of control."
"Of course you have to go to school today."	"It sounds like you wish it would snow, and they would have to cancel school for the day. Well, I'll tell you a secret: Sometimes I feel that way about going to work."

In each of the above examples, the parent is not going to give the child what the child wants. The difference is that in the case of the hard no, the child gets the feeling that the parent could not care less.

On the other hand, when the child receives the empathy of the feeling response, she feels like she has a companion to share her concerns and who is willing to help her solve her problems. This spirit of cooperation is a huge step in the direction of taming a spirited child. It establishes a tie, and as recent brain research suggests, such human interaction actually reshapes the neural connections of the brain.

Limits

The second step of the FLAC method, *L*, stands for "limits." After acknowledging the validity of your child's feelings about the situation, you want to remind him gently of the limits that you are operating under. The limits may refer to family rules or other corrals that we discussed in chapter 6, or it may simply be the needs of the situation as perceived by you the parent or by your youngster's teacher. While we are quite willing to grant the child any feelings that he may have and empathize with his desires, the reality of life is that we cannot always get what we want. In step one, we may grant him what he wants in fantasy ("You wish it would snow, and they would have to cancel school"), but in step two we need to remind him that the sky is blue, and we'd better get ready for school. This reality check may seem like a cold slap in the face after the warm fuzzy of the empathy step, but if you are gentle and continue the spirit of cooperation, then it is not likely to interfere with the relationship building that is underway. If your desire is sincere, then your voice and body language will communicate caring and pave the way to step three. Before we go there, however, let's take another look at the feeling-response examples from earlier and add some possible limit-setting transitions. Again, put yourself in the child's shoes and see how you would feel if your parent spoke to you like this:

FEELING RESPONSE	LIMIT SETTING
"It's hard to go to bed when you're not feeling very sleepy."	"But you still need your sleep to grow healthy and strong."
"Those cookies are really good, aren't they? I wish I could eat a dozen of them!"	"But if I did, I probably would blow up like a big balloon!"
"You really enjoy your bath time, don't you?"	"Sometimes I think you'd like to come back as a fish and swim all day long. But it's close to bedtime, and I still want to read you a story."
"You are really frustrated right now. It feels like everything is out of control."	"I wonder how you can calm yourself down."
"It sounds like you wish it would snow, and they would have to cancel school for the day. Well, I'll tell you a secret: Sometimes I feel that way about going to work."	"But the sky looks pretty blue to me, so I guess we both need to get ready to go."

Would you feel like your parent was your enemy or an understanding leader if you were the child in the above situations? Chances are that you would feel pretty good about working with such a parent to find a solution to your problem. A little empathy goes a long way when it comes to accepting reality. You may not get what you want, but at least you have a big person on your side that understands and supports you. That makes it a whole lot easier to accept what you cannot change.

Alternatives

The *A* in FLAC stands for "alternatives." When parents refuse spirited children what they want or require them to do what they do not want, there is a terrible tendency to make their words final. It is as if the parent were to say to the child "No, you can't have what you want," and

- tough luck.
- grin and bear it.
- get used to it.
- who said life was fair?
- don't bother me about it.
- shut up.
- what are you going to do about it, huh?

Of course, sophisticated parents do not use these words. But their tone of voice and facial expressions may convey the same attitude. These hard no's almost invite a spirited child into a struggle for power. On the other hand, by establishing some empathy for the child with a feeling response and then gently reminding the child of the situation's limits, the parent has a wonderful opportunity to build on the positive relationship by offering an alternative to what the child desires.

A good alternative is the sweetest consolation prize ever invented. In fact, we have all experienced alternatives that turned out to be even better than what we had first wanted. Children who see their parents as willing to provide or negotiate reasonable alternatives when what they want is outside the corral also see their parents as partners in helping them find happiness. "She does care about how I feel and what I want. She wasn't just spouting words she learned in a parenting book; she really does want me to be happy." The idea that we want our kids to be happy is a powerful force in winning cooperation *if*—I repeat, *if*—you do not go overboard and indulge your child with bribes and other alternatives that should be off-limits as well. For example, a parent who says no to the child who wants a sweet before dinner, only to let the child watch an extra hour of television as compensation, is teaching the child to manipulate. A better alternative would be to offer the child a healthy snack before dinner ("How about some crunchy carrots or celery sticks to hold you over?") and then the promise of the desired sweet as dessert after a nutritious meal (if you do desserts in your family at all).

In our above example, Mother introduces the idea of looking at alternatives when she says:

"Well, I don't want you to wear something you hate. But we have to get going so you can get to school on time, and I can get to work. Got any ideas?"

The request for ideas invites her son into a partnership to find a solution to his problem. This attitude that "we are in this together" helps win his cooperation and find a solution at the same time. When Adam says that he would like to wear his pajama top, she does not shoot down the idea but recognizes that her son's hypersensitivity to fabrics might make the top's softness feel good against his skin. She acknowledges this fact with another feeling response:

"That top feels nice and soft, doesn't it? I can see why you'd like to wear it."

Again, by accepting his feelings, she keeps the spirit of cooperation building. She might go a step further and use this information to suggest another soft shirt, but one that would be appropriate for school. Instead, she uses humor to remind him of the limits of what is OK to wear at school, while at the same time suggesting another alternative:

"It would be pretty funny, too, you showing up in your pajamas while everyone else had on school clothes. Your teacher might just put you to bed. Now, maybe if they had a pajama day and everyone wore pj's on the same day, that would be cool."

She may not have meant the pajama day as a real alternative, but once it is on the table, and Adam jumps on it ("Yeah, can we?"), she does not back down but lets him know that she will follow up with his teacher to see if it's possible. At the same time, she reminds him of the reality of the situation and offers another alternative: a red shirt. Adam does not go for this alternative, and the give-and-take continues for a bit until a green shirt is decided upon. When looking for alternatives with your child, keep in mind that young children can usually be directed toward an alternative. For example:

- "The refrigerator is not for playing in. Here are some plastic containers that you can play with."
- "We don't use Pop-Tarts for art projects. Here is some Play-Doh for you to make art projects with."
- "The rule is no running in the house. Let's go outside, so that you can run around."

As children get older, looking for alternatives becomes more of a cooperative venture. You can make suggestions, but do not feel that it is up to you to come up with a solution. Kids who have been involved in such problem solving can be remarkably creative in finding innovative, and acceptable, alternatives to their problems. Learn to use phrases like the following to get the process going:

- "Let's see if we can come up with an alternative."
- "I have an idea."
- "What do you think about . . . ?"
- "What can you suggest?"
- "What else can you think of?"

When a suitable alternative is found, it is a small matter to put it into action. However, when nothing seems to please the child except for what is outside the limits, remember that the key to avoiding power struggles is to neither fight nor give in. It is therefore important that you not give in and give him the cookie, and so on. Giving in to unreasonable alternatives (that is, demands) will encourage the child to rebel more in the future. After all, if refusing to accept compromise gets the other person to back down, then the child learns to be hardheaded about what he wants. Unfortunately, people who always have to have their own way are neither very happy or much of a pleasure to be around. The result of bending over backward for kids is more than a sore back for the parent to endure, it is a spoiled child for the world to endure. The reality that you can't always get what you want—and that even a good alternative is sometimes hard to find—is an important lesson for children to learn. When your child continues to resist any attempt to find an acceptable alternative, you can move on to step four of the FLAC method: consequences.

Consequences

When moving from feelings, limits, and alternatives to consequences, be sure that you move on gently and kindly, not with anger and resentment for having all of your good alternatives rejected by this persnickety child. As I said in the last chapter, consequences that are used in anger with a powerful child will almost always backfire. The child will resent your attitude and dig in her heels harder to show you that you cannot run over her that way. If you stay friendly and let the consequences flow logically from the impasse that exists, your child may find the added incentive of avoiding a logical consequence enough to agree to one of the alternatives. Mother achieved this in the opening example by introducing the logical consequence of missing a good breakfast when she said:

"Wow, we are running out of options, and if we don't get downstairs in five minutes, we'll miss breakfast and have to eat something quick in the car. So let me ask you, which of the shirts in your drawer do you hate least?"

"The green one, I guess."

"Then the green one it is!" said Mom cheerfully as she put it down in front of her son.

The desire to have a good breakfast instead of a plain piece of bread and cheese in the car helped Adam make up his mind. Mother's tone stayed friendly, and, in fact, she used a little humor to keep things light when she asked which shirt he hated least. Of course, if her son was not a breakfast eater, this logical consequence would not have provided much motivation. But remember that there are as many logical consequences as you and your child can think of, so look for something that you think will matter to your child. For example, Mother could have also said one of the following:

- "If we do not get going, we'll be late, and that means we will have to go to bed earlier tonight so we can get up earlier tomorrow and figure out what to wear."

- "I'll set the timer for one minute, and if you can pick a shirt to wear before it goes off, you get to choose. But if it goes off before you have chosen, then I'll chose one for you."

- "Adam, I know how much you enjoy watching a few minutes of *Veggie Tales* while I'm making breakfast, so pick one of these shirts before the timer goes off, and you will still have time to watch. Otherwise, we'll have to hurry out the door and eat a piece of bread in the car." This is not a bribe as long as watching *Veggie Tales* is a normal part of the morning routine. And remember, it is handy to always build in some fun things in any routine so that if the child balks at one point, he loses out on the rest of the routine, including the fun parts.

You may have already noticed that this particular problem could have been avoided altogether with a little forethought. If Mom and Adam had laid out his school clothes the night before, it is unlikely that he would have resisted putting on the shirt that morning. We will talk more about the important area of problem prevention in chapter 10. But even with the best prevention efforts, there will be times when you need to discipline your child, and the FLAC method is the best that I've come up with in thirty years of working with parents.

Family Meetings

The FLAC method is usually used spontaneously when problems arise. However, many proactive families have instituted regular family meetings for handling problems that emerge during the week and heading off others before they occur. These meetings can be scheduled on short notice ("I think we need a family meeting to discuss this. How about tonight after dinner?"), or they can be held once a week at a specific time. ("It's three o'clock on Sunday. Time for our family meeting.") Meetings can be elaborate, with official minutes, rotating chairpersons, old business, new business, and a shared snack and/or game at the end, or simplified as you choose.

One way to get any meeting off to a good start is to begin by sharing compliments. This is a time when anyone in the family can share a compliment or appreciation for any other family member. Parents usually set the tone by offering their own compliments, but over time the kids will learn how to give as well as receive. I know it sounds a little hokey, but it works surprisingly well.

The main part of the meeting is to problem solve issues that arise during the week. These issues are put on an agenda during the week by any family member who has a problem to resolve. The agenda is nothing more than a blank sheet of paper labeled "Agenda" and taped to the refrigerator or other "public" place. Children as well as adults are encouraged to put items on the agenda that they want to discuss. Then during the meeting, the chair brings up the first item on the agenda and covers as many as time allows. Speaking of time, keep your meetings relatively brief so as not to burn out the kids on meetings. Twenty minutes maximum for young children and up to about forty minutes for older ones is enough.

When an item is brought up for discussion, use a modification of the four steps of the FLAC method to find a solution:

1. The person who writes the item on the agenda is asked if the problem still exists. Many times kids will work out things on their own once they know there is a family forum that will handle it if they do not. If the problem still exists, the person is asked to describe the problem, being careful to be respectful of others.

2. Ask everyone to share thoughts and feelings about the issue.

3. Brainstorm possible alternatives for solving the problem, including logical consequences if necessary for future use.

4. Decide on a solution that everyone can live with. Although this type of consensus problem solving takes a little longer, it is better than voting in that no one feels ganged up on.

5. Write down the agreement, so that everyone's memory is the same, and then review this at the next meeting to see if it is going well. If there is still a problem, begin again and look for a new solution.

Family meetings take some getting used to, but those families that make them a habit find that they pay multiple benefits and are well worth the time.

9

A Lump of Sugar Called Encouragement

Children need encouragement like plants need water.

—RUDOLF DREIKURS, MD

(1897–1972), American psychia-

trist, author, educator

SEVEN-YEAR-OLD RANDALL HAD been in a power struggle with his dad over going to bed for some time. His father had recently changed tactics from yelling and punishing to using a combination of logical consequences and the FLAC method. Together they had worked out an agreement that Randall would get into bed at eight o'clock, and his mom or dad would read him a story for twenty minutes. After the story, they would turn off the light and say prayers. Then if Randall wanted, his parent on duty that night would scratch his back for a few minutes and then kiss him good night with a gentle "I love you."

Three-year-old Demetria refused to put away her toys when her mother asked. No amount of polite requests, firm reminders, or I messages seemed to help. Finally Mom tried a logical consequence using a when-then choice: "When you have put away your toys, Demetria, then we will have our afternoon snack." Demetria didn't have to think twice, and as she started putting toys in the toy box, her mother said, "Wow, Demetria, you are really good at putting your toys in the box. And your room is looking really great! Come on, and you can help me make your snack."

Ten-year-old William had finally decided to comply with his parents' wishes and stick to his homework until he was finished. They had worked out an alternative for him to do it right after dinner instead of when he got home from school, and he appreciated the time to play before having to buckle down. But now that he was doing his work well, they seemed to ignore his effort. Didn't they notice how much better he was doing? Why didn't they say anything? After a few days of this, William decided, "What's the use? They don't appreciate what I do anyway, and besides, they only notice me when I misbehave. Forget this!" The next thing his parents noticed was William playing video games while his half-finished homework lay on the kitchen table.

Each of the parents in these three examples did a good job of using the discipline skills presented in the previous three chapters. But discipline by itself is seldom enough to create lasting change. Something else is needed, something to sweeten the deal. Something that makes it truly a win-win experience for both parents and child. By now, I hope you know that I am not talking about rewards or bribes. If you resort to such tangible incentives, you may as well just pay kids to behave well. You will get the behavioral results that you want in the short run, but you will be creating a "What's in it for me?" monster in the process. A kid raised on reward and manipulation has a hard time making the transition from doing the right thing for a payoff to doing the right thing because he is a person of character and integrity. Raising children is a lot more than just getting good behavior. It is also about developing good people.

The types of sweetener that I am suggesting springs much more from the developing relationship between you and your child than from any outside reward. A word of appreciation, a positive comment, a pat on the back, a kiss, a little extra attention, being invited to help make the snack with Mommy—this is the stuff that means the most to children at a deep level. This is the stuff that builds courage and self-esteem while reinforcing positive behavior. Without it, kids are like plants thirsting for water and withering in the sun. Your encouragement to your spirited child for positive effort, improvement, and success is like the lump of sugar that a horse wrangler might use to tame a wild horse. In fact, even a horse wrangler knows to add an encouraging word along with the lump of sugar, so that the horse eventually learns to respond to the words alone.

Children, who are a lot smarter than horses, require more subtlety. Instead of tangible rewards, look for activities that are positive in and of themselves. The reading time and back scratching that Randall's parents employed to make bedtime more palatable are reasonable activities whether or not he was having trouble going to bed. As such, they do not run the risk of teaching him to manipulate to get what he wants. When Demetria's mother sets up a when-then choice for her daughter, she is not bribing her with a snack, because a snack occurs every afternoon anyway. She simply orders things so that the toys must be picked up before snack time. But she does not leave it at that. Once Demetria is motivated to pick up her toys, Mother looks for an opportunity to praise her. This makes the effort of putting toys away even more worthwhile and more likely to happen again next time.

Courage and the Spirited Heart

Your child craves your recognition and encouragement. Even a spirited child who keeps his parents busy with power struggles, fits of anger, and bouts of sensitivity wants that special encouragement that only a parent can give—the encouragement that says, "You are doing well," "You are making progress," "I am glad you are my child." Why do children yearn for our recognition and support? We could look to psychology for some answers and discuss how their birth into a relatively helpless state makes them dependent on us for their survival and sets up a lifelong struggle to gain competence and independence. We could talk about how a striving for significance motivates children to look to us not only to meet their physical needs but to validate that they are moving in a positive direction as contributing members of the family and community.

Like I said, we *could* look to psychology, but instead let's look at semantics. For centuries, the heart has been considered the special center of the human spirit. From King Richard the Lionheart to the Broadway show tune "Heart," the word *heart* has been used to connote the attributes of courage, love, and intestinal fortitude. The spirited horse Seabiscuit was reputed to be a small horse with a lot of heart who beat out the much bigger horse War Admiral, who presumably had less heart. In every culture, the heart has been revered as a special organ that has a larger-than-life meaning. In fact, the French word *coeur*, meaning *heart*, became the English word *courage*. And courage, according to both the pioneering Austrian psychiatrist Alfred Adler and the heroic English prime minister Winston Churchill, is the most important human quality because it is the one quality upon which all the others rest. Everything takes courage, because there is risk involved in all endeavors. Without adequate courage, children give in to their fears and attempt to meet their goals in easier ways—often turning to misbehavior.

For example, without the courage to work hard in school to overcome a challenging course, the child's fear can turn him toward apathy and giving up. Without the courage to learn how to get along with others, a child may revert to his easier aggressive nature and seek to dominate others. Without the courage to do without what he desires, the child may become demanding and rebellious, always attempting to have his own way. Without a doubt, spirited children need a healthy reservoir of courage if they are to grow into productive, successful, contributing members of their family and community. Therefore, one of our most important jobs as parents is to provide the sweet taste of encouragement as our spirited children work toward success and change.

Parents as Encouragers and Discouragers

Continuing with a little semantics, parents can either instill courage in their children (en-courage) or remove courage (dis-courage). It would be nice to think that we are interested only in encouraging our children, but the fact is that we do both, and there is no way around it. Even the most well-meaning parent at times discourages her child. The trick is to reduce the amount of discouragement that we give and increase the amount of encouragement.

Why can't we just eliminate discouragement altogether? The answer is that encouragement and discouragement are in the mind of the beholder. Take, for example, a parent's compliment: "You look great in that dress, sweetie!" What one child might experience as encouraging ("I like to look good, and I guess I do in this dress"), another might interpret as discouraging ("You're just saying that because I gave you such a hard time about wearing it. The dress still looks stupid, and now so do I!").

To complicate things even more, the same child can respond differently to the same communication on two different days just because of what is happening to her on those days and her ensuing mind-set. Add to this that we adults also have our own ups and downs, experiences, and mind-sets. We can let discouraging comments slip without even thinking at those times. All of this makes the critical job of encouragement a skill that takes a lot of practice. As with most skills, begin with an increased awareness of what you are doing and try to refrain from saying or doing things that will discourage your child.

Remember, when children become discouraged, they are more likely to resort to misbehavior to meet their needs. The more we put them down and criticize, the worse they feel about themselves, and the more discouraged they become. They begin to think that they cannot do anything right, so why bother trying? Instead they resort to easier, negative behavior to get what they want. If the parent responds with more punishment, criticism, and discouragement, the child just spirals downward until both parent and child are hopelessly discouraged.

Let's look at some typical ways that parents of spirited children often discourage their children:

- **Parents discourage when they focus on mistakes and misbehavior; when they expect the worst from their child and when nothing the child does is good enough.** Part of our job as parents is to help our children learn from their mistakes and be more successful in the future. This includes correcting their misbehavior. This in itself is not necessarily discouraging. What discourages children is when they hear more about what they are doing wrong than what they are doing right. When we focus our attention on their problems and ignore the positives, kids begin to feel there is more wrong with them than right. This becomes terribly discouraging. When our attitude is "Mistakes are bad, and you are worth less when you make them; stop being such a problem child and clean up your act," kids lose courage and become afraid of messing up. To compensate, they either stop trying to improve (after all, what's the point if we never notice?), or they retaliate against us by misbehaving even more. When we communicate that we expect our kids to misbehave or mess up, they often become discouraged and live down to our expectations. When we constantly raise the bar on them so that nothing they do ever feels acceptable, this too is discouraging.

- **Parents encourage when they build on strengths, show confidence, and accept their child for who she is.** Instead of focusing on mistakes and misbehavior, parents can learn to build on their child's strengths and successes. A better attitude for parents to hold is this: "Mistakes are for learning. See what you can learn from this one and how to improve in the future." When we show patience for our spirited child's struggle and take the time to correct misbehavior respectfully without rancor or insult, we set the stage for courageous effort on their part. When we show confidence that they can and will succeed, they learn to believe in themselves and give additional effort to improving. After all, "If mom and dad believe I can improve, then maybe I can!"

In addition to a positive approach to discipline, parents also need to work at overcoming the "homeostasis problem." What I mean by this is that our bodies are geared to notice things when they get out of kilter. If the temperature gets too hot or too cold in the room, we notice. But as long as we are comfortable, we are oblivious. This is great for getting along with nature, but it sucks when applied to our relationships with other people, especially our children. Kids need to hear from us about five times more encouragement than criticism, even constructive criticism. This means that we have to notice their strengths and positive efforts. Then by expressing our appreciation for these attitudes, traits, and behaviors, we increase courage and more positive behavior. This is encouragement. Consider some of the following statements, and imagine if you were the child hearing them from your parent:

- "Thanks for helping with the dishes. You were a big help."
- "I like the way you shared with your sister. That was very generous of you."
- "I love the way that your whole face lights up when you smile."
- "You have a quick mind, Jenny."
- "You are really good at this towel-folding business, Ken. Thanks for helping me."
- "Nice coloring, Susan."
- "Say, I've noticed that you have kept your cool for three days in a row. Way to go, Stephen."
- "I could see you getting a little frustrated with putting on those new shoes, but you didn't let it throw you, and you kept at it until you got it. That kind of sticking with it will take you a long way, Adrianne."
- "You have a great sense of humor, Ben."
- "If I haven't told you lately, I'm really glad that you are my daughter."

Chances are that if you were the child in each of these examples, you would feel a little bit better about yourself and your parent. You would feel encouraged to try even harder in the future and be willing to work cooperatively with your mom or dad. In fact, encouragement is such a powerful motivator that with a little planning it can be very effective at changing behavior, as the following story demonstrates.

The Amazing Story of the Impertinent Freshmen Psychology Class

Once upon a time there was a professor who gave the most inspiring lectures about the power of encouragement to his freshmen psychology class. He would dutifully stand behind his lectern and lecture on the undeniable power of even the subtlest forms of encouragement such as mere attention. In fact, he taught his students that what is noticed by a parent increases, while what is ignored often goes away. If you only notice misbehavior and mistakes, that is what you will get. But if you downplay those behaviors and notice the positive things your child does, you will see more of that in the future.

The class was impressed. They were also a little intrigued and decided to try an experiment of their own to see if the professor's words were as wise as they seemed. So here's what they did, the little imps: They decided they would attempt to get the professor to move from his rigid position behind the lectern by paying attention whenever he took a step away from the safety of his wooden perch. When he stepped away, they would look interested, take notes, and nod their heads approvingly. This sort of thing is highly encouraging to professors. If he happened to drift back toward the lectern, they would look away, yawn, and appear disinterested. In less than a single class period, they had successfully trained their professor to lecture from the opposite end of the stage, ten feet away from his podium. And the amazing part of the experiment is that he did not even know they had done it! They had subtly changed his behavior by nothing more than systematically encouraging step-by-step progress in the direction they wanted him to move. Then, of course, being freshmen, they gave it all away by bursting into laughter—while the startled professor, checking his zipper, wondered what was so hilarious.

Encouraging Positive Change: The SUGAR Method

To help you apply the simple wisdom demonstrated by the psychology professor's astute students, try using a little sugar of your own. This acronym for motivating positive behavior change stands for:

S: Small steps.

U: Use encouraging words.

G: Go for the next step.

A: Acknowledge strengths, effort, progress, and successes.

R: Repeat as necessary.

You do not need to memorize this formula and use it religiously. Simply learning to include the steps in your efforts to encourage your child will provide rich results even if you leave out a step or two along the way. However, to clarify the process, let's look at each step more closely.

S: Small Steps

The secret to accomplishing large goals is to never try to accomplish large goals. Large goals are just too frustrating to pursue, and people inevitably give up before they achieve them. Instead, break down large goals into small goals and take it one step at a time.

It is analogous to teaching a baby to walk. You do not prop her up against the wall across the room and say "Come walk over here, honey." You know that to do so would be folly. She would stumble a step or two and then ignominiously fall on her rump. Instead you offer her both physical and emotional support as she walks a single step, then two steps, then three, until she toddles across the room on her own. And then from that day on you try to catch her, but that's another story.

The same principle applies to teaching your child anything, from a sports skill to academics to better behavior and even character. Do not expect your child to change in one giant leap, but break down the large goal into baby steps. This provides many opportunities for your child to succeed along the way, and as the old saying goes, "Nothing succeeds like success." The more we succeed, the more encouraged we are to keep trying, and so the more we succeed in the future. The same is true for your spirited child. A "success cycle" is a parent's dream, as the child builds from success to success, handling problems with energy and motivation, and continuing to thrive.

For example, eight-year-old Carlos was very competitive at board games. He loved to win, and when the game was not going his way, he would become frustrated and often lose his temper. On one occasion, he trashed a perfectly good Monopoly set after landing on Marvin Gardens with a hotel. His parents wanted to teach their son how to be a good sport and to play without getting upset and having a tantrum. Recognizing that this goal was too big to attempt at once, they broke it down into a number of small steps so that he could experience the sweet taste of success many times along the way:

1. They talked with Carlos about the importance of being a good sport. Specifically, they discussed with him that it was more important to play well than to win. Once he agreed to work on staying calm when things were not going well, they moved on to step two.

2. They broke down the game into ten-minute periods and focused on staying "calm, cool, and collected" for a single period at a time. This really became five or six steps, as a game lasted about an hour.

3. As Carlos began having more and more successful periods of sportsmanlike behavior, his parents shifted the focus to playing full games without losing his cool. They took it a game at a time, building up to more and more games without an outburst.

There is no precise formula for planning baby steps. Talk it over with your child, partner, or another support person and think creatively. Make it easy to succeed and keep building on those successes.

Of course, not every step will be met with success. Stagnation and even backsliding will occur. Progress is like the stock market: up and down and up and down, but always in a positive upward trend. The key is for you to not let yourself or your child become discouraged and give up after a setback. Think of these setbacks as part of the learning process and teach your child that mistakes are for learning. Then look for the next opportunity to succeed.

U: Use Encouraging Language

Your encouraging words, tone of voice, facial expressions, body language, and even underlying attitude can convey either an air of encouragement or discouragement to your child. When your communication is encouraging, it is like sugar to your child's tongue, motivating her to continue to progress toward each step of her goal. Learn to use words that convey an attitude of confidence in your child's ability to succeed and to stick with it when the going gets hard, and that show an acceptance for your child regardless of the outcome. If you did not hear a lot of encouragement growing up yourself, this may be a challenge, and you will have to concentrate on developing an encouraging attitude and finding the right words. Be patient with yourself, and encouraging. You are learning, too, and you will make mistakes. Catch yourself with a smile instead of a kick and look for ways to communicate encouragement at the next opportunity.

When Carlos played Monopoly with his parents the next time after they had talked with him about the need for good sportsmanship, they followed up with a lot of encouragement. For example:

"Nice job keeping your cool when you landed on my property, Carlos."

"I'm really enjoying your company."

"I know it can be frustrating when the dice don't come up with a good number, but you are really handling it well."

"Ooo, that hurts, but you really played a good game. And we had fun together, which is what counts!"

Along with their encouraging words, Carlos's mother and father smiled a lot at him, touched him affectionately, and laughed with him. If he started to become frustrated or show temper they gently reminded him, "You can handle it. Keep your cool, Carlos."

G: Go for the Next Step

You may believe that the most powerful force in the universe is your child's spirited CAPPS when unleashed, and you may be right. The curiosity, adventurousness, power, persistence, and sensitivity that tend to make everything about your child more intense are extremely powerful. However, an opposing force called inertia can keep things from changing with an incredible power of its own.

In physics, inertia is the tendency of "a body at rest to remain at rest." I realize that your spirited child seems to never need rest until he falls asleep exhausted on the floor. However, inertia tends to work against change as well as against physical movement. People tend to do what they are used to doing, and taking a step in a new direction is difficult. It is easy to try, meet with some obstacle, become discouraged, and give up. The state of giving up is inertia, a trip back to the status quo. Sometimes a fear of failure or of the effort required to make a change can also lock a child into an inert state. Finding the courage to forge ahead can be difficult. This is a time when a parent's encouragement can give the child the psychological energy to move forward.

Carlos may decide that he wants to control his anger rather than have his anger control him. Yet when he is in a difficult situation, and feelings of frustration begin to mount, he may find it hard to make the effort to keep progressing. By encouraging him to keep trying, his parents can be the difference between his giving in to defeat or moving through this gray area toward success. For example:

"I know this is frustrating, Carlos, but let's take three deep breaths together and cool ourselves down."

"Math can be frustrating, Fran, but if you keep at it, I know you will get it. Let's take a short break, then we'll tackle this next problem."

"You did a great job staying with me at the convenience store yesterday, Todd. Are you ready to tackle the big grocery store today and help me pick out the food for the week?" (And yes, that does include picking out desserts, because sometimes sugar is still just sugar.)

A: Acknowledge Strengths, Progress, and Results

As I wrote earlier, when a horse moves in the direction that the wrangler wants, progressing toward the ultimate goal of taming, she gets a lump of sugar. Your acknowledgement is a sweet bit of psychological sugar that can provide the encouragement for your child to keep moving toward the goal. So many parents who rely on anger, criticism, and punishment to change behavior would be amazed at how much more powerful a simple "attaboy," "attagirl," or pat on the back can be. Training ourselves to acknowledge our children's strengths, efforts, progress, and results is no easy task, but the more we "catch 'em doing good" instead of bad, the more we sweeten the deal in letting us tame them.

Be sure to notice that it is not enough to just wait and acknowledge results, even of small steps. We also focus our acknowledgement on the strengths that our child brings to the task. You can especially focus on the five CAPPS of spirited children and give them credit for the positive aspects of these traits. For example:

Curious: "You are really good at investigating things, Robert. I bet if

171

you turn that keen mind of yours onto this problem, you'll find a solution."

Adventurous: "You really like to try new things, Susan. Let's explore some ways you can relax yourself at night so you can get to sleep better."

Powerful: "I really like how powerful you are, Carlos. When you use that power in a calm, cool, and collected way, you really make things happen!"

Persistent: "You are really good at sticking with something that catches your attention, Daniel. That's going to be a big help to you on this project."

Sensitive: "You are a very sensitive person, Gail, and that will help you know what others are feeling, so that you can be a good friend. What do you think Charlene was feeling when she said that to you?"

It is especially important to acknowledge effort as they work toward completing a step:

"I can see how hard you are working at this, Camille. Keep it up, and you'll get it."

"I like the way you try, Darnell. That shows me you really care."

"You are really working hard on getting your room in order, Max. Nice going!"

"I can see how hard you are working at keeping calm, Carlos. Way to go!"

And progress:

"Your room is looking much better, Max. Just a little more, and you'll have it done."

"You've finished half your math problems, Darnell. Way to go!"

"Carlos, that's the third game of Monopoly in a row that you have been a pleasure to play with!"

R: Repeat as Necessary

Sometimes, despite everyone's best efforts, change is slow to occur, and it is easy to feel discouraged. Take heart! You can dig deep into your own reserves of courage and start over. Rethink the "small steps." Maybe you need to find some even smaller steps to build in some successes that will motivate continued effort. Think about how your efforts at using "encouraging communication" are coming across to your child. Remember that what you may intend to be encouraging may be experienced by your child as discouraging. Do you need to change your words? Maybe your tone of voice is too syrupy and comes across as patronizing. If so, try being more matter of fact. Are you hovering over your child like a helicopter? Maybe you need to back off a little and give him room to work more on his own.

Some kids actually react negatively to too much encouragement and see it as phony, an attempt to manipulate them. Sometimes fewer words is better. Even a backhanded "not too shabby" can be a way to get through. Try using no words at all, just a thumbs-up sign, a wink, or a touch on the shoulder. Experiment to see what encourages *your* child. And don't give up. No matter how your child responds outwardly, he needs to know that you believe in him, love him, and value him as the special gift that he is. This is the core of taming: of establishing ties.

Letters from Heaven

When I was in my early twenties, I found a box of old memorabilia. Going through the faded photographs of grandparents and trips long since forgotten, I came across a small stack of letters written to me by my mother. I had never seen them before and didn't even know where they came from. I only knew that I felt compelled to read them.

The letters talked about many things, like her ongoing illness and how much she missed the family. But they also talked to me directly. They told of a mother's love for her son and how proud she was of the person I was becoming. They focused on specific strengths she had seen in me: my abilities on the basketball court and in school, my efforts at creative writing, and the gentle person she saw me as. As I read on, I felt the bond between us strengthen almost as if she were still alive. She had died several years earlier when I was seventeen, and though I had no idea where these letters had come from, it was as if they had been written from heaven.

A short time later, as a young Sunday school teacher, I decided at the end of the year to write my students letters focusing on their individual strengths and areas in which I had seen them improve. As they left for summer vacation, I handed each of them their letter and then thought no more about the gesture for four years. It was then that I attended a reception one night and ran into a woman who introduced herself as the mother of one of my students from that class. "You know that letter you wrote to Alice?" she said. "Well, I want you to know that she still has it pinned to her bulletin board."

Putting our encouragement into writing seems to make it extra special. Our kids can savor the words at their own speed, rereading them as they please whenever they need a lift of spirit. I have been asking parents to write these letters of encouragement for thirty years now, and the stories they tell me of how powerful they are has made me believe that they are truly special to children, almost like a letter from heaven.

A father once wrote me that he had been estranged from his teenage daughter for several years because of problems during her adolescence. He had enrolled in my *Active Parenting of Teens* course in hopes of preventing the same thing from happening with his younger daughter. When the group came to the assignment about writing a letter of encouragement, he decided also to write his estranged daughter, who was now living a thousand miles away. The daughter was so moved by his outpouring of encouragement that she wrote back, and their relationship was healed, almost miraculously. Tragically, the daughter died a couple of years later from a rare illness, which prompted the father to write me. He shared that his reconciliation with his daughter was what helped him through his tragic loss, and had she died while still estranged, he would never have forgiven himself.

The power of encouragement when put in writing is a mysterious phenomenon. You may not experience the response overtly from your child, but trust that your words will hit home and come back to strengthen the relationship and your child's sense of self in many, many ways for years to come. A few simple tips may help, but let the letter come from your heart to your child's heart, and you can't go wrong:

- Write about specific areas of improvement or success, not generalities.
- Share only things that you like about him.
- Be honest and sincere.
- Mention how his behavior has been helpful to others.
- Let her know how glad you are that she is your daughter.

The goal of encouragement is not to heap massive amounts of undeserved praise on your tiny child's shoulders. It will weigh her down with false expectations and give her a sense of entitlement that can cause pain to herself and others. Instead, use encouragement wisely. Sure, kids need encouragement like plants need water, but too much water can rot the roots. Compliment your child's behavior, not your child's personality. Do not label your child a good boy, bad boy, smart girl, dumb girl, or anything else. Negative labels tend to stick and produce more negative behavior. Positive labels can spoil and lead to an inflated sense of self. Focusing on behavior and attitude gives the child something he can work on and feel good about earning.

Anger, Tantrums, and the Rustling of Reason

> When anger rises, think of the consequences.
> —CONFUCIUS
> (551 BC–479 BC)

> Usually when people are sad, they don't do anything. They just
> cry over their condition. But when they get angry, they bring about
> a change.
> —MALCOLM X (1925–1965),
> Malcolm X Speaks (1965)

WHEN SPIRITED CHILDREN are overtaken with emotion the expression is often ugly and vile. Eyes flooded with tears, they may yell at you, hurling insults that appall you with their venom and vulgarity. They may even wish that you were dead. It is hard not to take such behavior personally, but it is not personal. They have gone well beyond the personal into a part of the brain where primitive forces still rule. They lash out at you, because it is you who have stood in their way preventing them from getting what they want when they want it. Or maybe you have only tried to calm them when something outside has frustrated them, and they turn their frustration toward you. You are the object of their wrath, but their pain goes well beyond you and the limits you have set. The tears come from a secret place that feels such overwhelming frustration at the moment that many of the social inhibitions they have learned are swept aside. They say and do things they know better than to say or do. They melt down in a heap of tears, feeling impotent and alone, their brain torn asunder by a flood of emotion they do not know how to control.

It is hard to reach a child at such times, but she needs you to reach her. She needs your constant love and acceptance, even as you continue to stand firm in your values about what is and is not acceptable behavior. She needs to know that no matter what, you will find a way to walk hand in hand with her again.

What Is Anger?

Anger is a confusing emotion. It has baffled theologians, philosophers, psychologists, and parents for the history of humankind. On the one hand, it seems so destructive. On the other, it must have some value to have lasted for so long. Parents of spirited children know the results of their children's tantrums—tantrums that often seem to go on for a good part of human history themselves. When our children lose control and give in to those powerful forces that seem to lie beyond reason, what can we do to minimize the damage and return them to normalcy? Better yet, how can we prevent these outbursts in the first place? And what of our own anger? How can we rein in the same destructive forces in ourselves? This chapter will give you some ideas and tools for handling these and other questions of the mysterious red rage.

Four-year-old Katrina could be a hurricane when things were not going her way. Her tantrums could last hours, and her parents had taken to walking on eggshells when they were around her.

Eight-year-old Kyle had very few friends, and it was no wonder. He was so easily angered that the other boys kept their distance for fear they would set him off.

Thirty-eight-year-old Dennis knew that his rage at his children's misbehavior only made matters worse. Still, when they continued to make the same mistakes over and over, what was he supposed to do, give them a cookie? At least he got it out instead of suffering in silence like *his* mother had done.

Anger, at its heart, is about problem solving. First, it provides motivation and energy for solving a problem. Second, it provides an evaluation of how well our problem-solving strategies are working. And third, when expressed through behavior, it has the capacity to be a problem-solving strategy itself. This is the positive side of anger. This is the anger that Malcolm X suggested can bring about positive change as it leads to solutions to human problems.

Anger is also one of the most destructive emotions. It is the force that leads to aggressive words and actions that often make problems worse and damage relationships. These are the consequences that Confucius talked about. So, in balance, is anger good or bad?

The problem, as with many problems, occurs when a little bit of a good thing becomes too much and overwhelms the system. A little bit of anger tells us there is a problem that needs addressing, gives us an energy boost to solve the problem, offers useful feedback along the way as we attempt to solve the problem, and can even send a firm message to others that we want them to change their behavior. Too much anger attacks the brain, rustling away our reasoning abilities like masked cowboys stealing cattle in the night. When anger (or fear, for that matter) overtakes our mental processes, we lose the ability to think rationally and revert to primitive means of settling problems. We yell, scream, threaten, sometimes hit, and in extreme cases, even kill. Later, when the flood of emotions subsides, and our rustled intellect is returned, we see the damage we have done and hopefully feel remorse.

Why do some people use anger quite effectively, while others seem to have "anger control problems," "short fuses," "lose it easily," "blow up," and have "anger issues"? The answer is usually a combination of genetics and experience. We all have a point at which we will become angry. For some this threshold is pretty low, taking very little to set them off. For others it is quite high, requiring a great deal to arouse this emotion.

This threshold is most likely set genetically. It is part of our temperament, and spirited kids usually have a pretty low threshold. Early life experiences then interact with the brain to move this threshold up or down. What happens when the child cries aggressively? Does the parent attempt to soothe the child, or does the parent pull away or even react angrily? How is the young child treated when he behaves in ways that do not please the parent? Is he disciplined respectfully and with kindness, or is he treated unfairly, harshly, or even abused? When a child does not get what she wants and has a tantrum, do the parents give in to her demands? All of these experiences have an impact on how quickly the child will become angry and, perhaps more important, what action the child will take when she does.

The good news is that just as the anger switch can be altered negatively by experience, it can also be reset to higher threshold levels by positive parenting and other experiences. The purpose of this chapter is to help you teach your child (and maybe yourself) how to become slower to anger, how to reduce it once it does occur, and how to use anger positively rather than destructively.

Managing Your Own Brain First

Before you can really help your child with his anger problem, you have to make sure that your own reasoning faculties are not being rustled away by premature anger. Since the key to taming a spirited child is to establish ties, anger that is too intense and occurs too often can damage those ties and impede the taming process. When you blow up at your child for his misbehavior or mistakes, the following negative results often occur:

- Your child learns to either fear you or fight you—either of which is bad for the relationship.

- You model the use of anger as a method of solving problems, teaching your child to do the same.

- Your logical mind disengages, and you revert to primitive means of parenting, including yelling, threatening, punishing, and even hitting. These methods only make your child's behavior worse in the long run, as they further damage the relationship.

- You get an adrenaline rush that feels good. This emotional catharsis can be addictive and make it easier for you to blow up the next time.

- Your child wins the power struggle. Remember that the key to handling a power struggle is to neither fight nor give in. When you get angry and fight, you send the message to your child "Look how powerful you are. Even though you did not get your way, you made me mad! You control my emotions."

Although the remainder of this chapter will focus on helping you help your child learn to manage her anger, much of this information can also be used to help manage your own emotions. Specifically, I'll focus on three areas:

1. Preventing anger from taking over,
2. Calming down once it has,
3. Learning from the experience afterward.

The Think-Feel-Do Cycle

Before we tackle these three areas, it may be helpful to consider the relationship among four factors in our children's lives: outside events (including our own parenting behavior), plus their thinking, feeling, and behavior. The following diagram is a simplified illustration of this system:

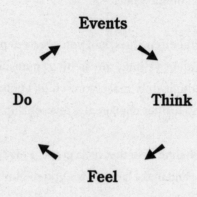

Event

Anything that happens in your child's awareness, conscious or otherwise, is an event. This could be a scary scene in a movie or you telling your child that he may not have a cookie before dinner. Following an event, your child may have an emotional reaction, such as, in the above two examples, fear or anger, respectively. There is a tendency to think that because an emotional reaction follows an event, the event itself caused the feeling. What the above model suggests, however, is that the event is first processed through the thinking brain.

Think

Thinking includes all of your child's conscious thoughts about the event as well as memories, attitudes, values, beliefs, and similar experiences of which she is not even aware at the moment, or at all. This vast network of experience is triggered by the event as electrochemical impulses in the brain begin to fire rapidly and make associations from this new event to everything that has been stored in memory that might be relevant. Like an iceberg, most of this thought process occurs beneath the surface, so that the child is unaware of what he is thinking.

Feel

What is thought, both consciously and subconsciously, triggers the child's emotional system, releasing brain chemicals that are experienced as joy, sadness, fear, hurt, and other feelings, including anger. It is important to note that the event does not *cause* the feeling, the feeling is caused by our thinking about the event. This is why two children can experience the same event in very different ways. One child may accept the denial of the cookie before dinner with mild disappointment, while another might experience intense frustration and anger.

Do

How a child responds to the event through his behavior can be as subtle as a blink of the eye, or as unsubtle as a full-fledged tantrum. This behavior is the result of an interaction among the child's thinking and feeling and the behavior itself, as ongoing feedback is processed very rapidly in the brain. The arrows on the model indicate that thinking, feeling, and doing are integrated in an ongoing feedback loop, as the child constantly evaluates his own responses and their effect on the event itself (Does Mom give in, or fight, or do something else?) and changes his thinking, feeling, and behavior to fit the new information. When this cycle is going well, problems are solved effectively, and positive results are maintained. However, when a child's experience has led him to draw some erroneous conclusions about events and how to change them, problems often get worse and repeat themselves.

There are two very important things to observe about the think-feel-do system:

1. Because it is a system, change at any point will filter throughout the entire system.
2. This means that if you want to reduce your child's anger, you can approach the problem through any of the four entry points: the event, or your child's thinking, feeling, or behavior. My suggestion is that you use all four entry points at different times to prevent, handle, and learn from an angry experience. Let's look at how.

Preventing Tantrums, Rage, and Other Over-the-Top Expressions of Anger

The old adage about an ounce of prevention being worth a pound of cure is highly applicable to spirited children and the problem of emotional rustling. When such kids get flooded with anger, they are extremely difficult to calm down. Any effort that you spend on preventing such experiences is therefore well worth the trouble, as long as you are not giving in to your child's unreasonable demands. Giving in to avoid a tantrum reinforces your child's tendency to have more tantrums in the future. To prevent emotional explosions without giving in, look at each of the four entry points of the system:

1. **Events.** You can minimize the chances of an event triggering an emotional overreaction in some of the following ways:

- Make sure that your own parenting is respectful, especially when disciplining. The methods presented in chapters 6 through 8 will help you make sure that you are not part of the problem. The FLAC method described in chapter 8, with its emphasis on feelings and alternatives is particularly recommended.

- Learn to notice when your child is beginning to become frustrated and offer to help him calm down, take a break, or use some other coping strategy.

- Help your child identify situations that tend to trigger frustration and anger. Then talk about how to avoid or cope with those situations as appropriate. For example, if she tends to lose it easily when she is tired, as many kids do, make sure that she gets on a good sleep schedule. If he has trouble staying calm when playing with his cousins over at Grandma's house, talk about this ahead of time and come up with some strategies for staying cool.

2. **Thinking.** Help your child become part of the solution by discussing anger with her and getting her to recognize the importance of keeping it under control. This does not mean that you want her to think that anger is bad or become ashamed of her anger, but you want her to keep the anger from overwhelming her and leading to destructive behavior. A good way to explain this to children of any age is to find a metaphor to which she can relate. For example:

- For younger kids: "Imagine that your anger is like a stove. When you are nice and calm, the stove is cool, and the color is gray. When something bothers you, it is like the stove gets turned on and starts to heat up and turns the color pink. When you get angrier, the stove gets hotter and turns a little red. If you don't do something about it when it gets red, it gets hotter and hotter and turns bright red. When this happens, it is so hot that you have to find a way to cool it off before it makes your problem worse. When something bothers you, I'll ask you, 'How hot is your stove now?' You can tell me it is cool gray, or a little pink, or getting red, or red hot! That way we'll both know how you feel and then think about what we can do to cool off and solve the problem."

Let your child know that anger can be a helpful emotion when he learns to listen to it when it first appears. "When your stove gets pink, that means that you have a problem to solve. Sometimes I may be able to help you, sometimes not. Try to solve the problem, but even if you don't solve it, it is important to keep yourself under control. That means not letting your stove get red hot. Let's talk about some things you can do to keep cool when your stove starts to heat up."

- For older kids: "Imagine that your anger is like one of those old-time thermometers with the big bulb at the bottom filled with a red liquid. Imagine that the bottom of the bulb is in your stomach, and the tube comes up your insides and out of your mouth. Got the picture?

  "Well, when you are nice and calm, that red stuff stays in the bottom. But when you get frustrated, it starts to bubble and rise—from a nice, calm 72 degrees to a very hot 212 degrees. Do you remember what 212 degrees means? Boiling! Have you ever been boiling mad? [Come up with an example together.] Yes, you were really angry that time. Well, the thing to remember is that a little anger is OK, because it can give us energy to solve problems. But when you let that red liquid stuff rise too high in the thermometer, it can come spurting out of your mouth and cause all sorts of worse problems. So the idea is to learn to listen to your thermometer when it first starts to bubble, and do something to handle the problem.

And if you can't solve the problem, then do something to stay calm. Because when you let your anger rise too high too fast, it tends to make a mess of things."

- Use your metaphor to help your child learn to gauge her anger. When she seems to be getting frustrated, ask her, "It looks like you are starting to heat up; how hot is your stove right now?" (Or "How hot is your thermometer right now?")

- Explain to your child that part of staying cool is being able to find alternatives when what you really want isn't possible right now. Nobody gets what he wants all of the time, but often he can find something else that will work. "Learn to ask yourself, 'What else could I do?'"

- Ask your child, "Who controls your anger: you or things outside of you? If you let things outside of you control you, then you are always at their mercy. But if you can learn to control your own anger, then you can learn to stay calm, cool, and collected no matter what happens. This gives you a lot of power in life."

- If you are a spiritual person, you might even teach older children the serenity prayer: "God grant me the serenity to accept the things I cannot change, the courage to change the things I can, and the wisdom to know the difference." If you don't want to make it a prayer, then find your own words to talk about accepting what you can't change.

- There are many children's books that deal with anger. Find one that you like and read it together. Then refer to it later when frustrating situations occur.

- Talk with your child about a "cool place" that she can go when she starts to overheat. This could be a special chair, a nook or cranny someplace, or even her bed. Later, when she starts to heat up, you can suggest she go to her cool place.

3. **Feeling.** The better your child is able to identify and express his feelings in words, the less likely he will be to act them out through misbehavior. The anger metaphor that you chose to use gives you a ready handle for making this feeling more real to your child. Use phrases and questions like the following to help your child learn to identify his anger early:

- "My stove is heating up right now. I think it's pretty pink. What about yours?"

- "How's your thermometer right now? Are you up to 100 degrees?"

- "Remember, when you get to 150 degrees, you go to boiling very fast, so let's start to bring it down a little."

- "Are you feeling tired?" (When kids feel tired, the anger-control manager inside their brains takes a nap!)

- "Are you feeling hungry?" (The same is true, on a lesser scale, with hunger. But keep your snacks healthy, as some kids react badly to too much sugar. Even for those who don't, sugar snacks interfere with good nutrition, which can cause other problems.)

- "I'm feeling very [fill in the blank here with whatever you are feeling, from disgusted to splendiferous]. How about you?" The idea is to help your child learn to identify and express a full range of emotions with words, facial expressions, and tone of voice.

4. **Do.** To prevent anger from escalating to the point that it takes over your child's system, experiment with the following to see what works best with your child:

- Make sure he gets enough sleep, nutrition, activity, and love.

- Offer a hug. "Can you use a hug right now?" (But don't insist!)

- "You seem to be heating up. Let's take some deep breaths together." Oxygen helps reduce anxiety, fear, anger, and other unpleasant emotions. Simple, slow, deep breaths can help return the system to normal. With older kids, you can teach them a more advanced form of breathing relaxation: the 1-4-2 ratio. This is one part inhale, four parts holding the breath, and two parts exhale. Multiplied by a factor of three seconds, this would mean three seconds in, twelve seconds hold, and six seconds exhale. Have your child close her eyes while you count out loud for her to follow. After three times through the cycle, have her hold for twenty seconds and then exhale hard. Then let her breathing return to normal while quietly focusing on the feeling of relaxation in her body. If 3-12-6 is too long for your child, try a factor of two, which would be two, eight, and four seconds.

- "Could you use a bath right now?" This sounds strange, but Mary Sheedy Kurcinka, in her wonderful book *Raising Your Spirited Child*, has found that spirited children are particularly calmed by water, especially bathing. Kurcinka reported that one mother, whose child was having an especially bad day, shared that her child had needed three baths that day! Other spirited kids seem to become relaxed when allowed to play with water in a sink with toys or pouring objects. Whatever magic water has to soothe the angry soul, experiment with it and see how your child can benefit.

- Ask her if she would like some time in her cool place, where she can cool down.

- Solve the problem. Work with your child to find a solution to his problem. You have set this up in your discussion about alternatives, so use that now. "What else can you do to solve your problem? What's a good alternative?"

- Do *not* fight or give in. I know I'm repeating this a lot, but it is critical that you avoid the temptation to get angry at your child and fuel the power struggle or give in to unreasonable demands to avoid her escalating her anger. Stay calm and respectful. It is OK to show some emotion, just do not let your own thermometer get over 100. If it starts to go higher, excuse yourself. "Honey, my own thermometer is getting a little hot right now. I'll be back when I've calmed down." This actually models anger management for your child as well as limits the power struggle.

- If your child is getting angry over your enforcement of limits or use of logical consequences, reassure her by saying, "It's OK, honey. You can try again later." Or "It's OK, there will be other opportunities."

- Use the FLAC method presented in chapter 8.

Tantrums: Heating Up and Cooling Down

Using the FLAC method (feelings, limits, alternatives, consequences) will reduce the likelihood of your child having a tantrum in response to your limit setting, but what if, despite your best efforts, anger does overwhelm his system? There are also many situations in which a tantrum is triggered by frustration at achieving a goal that has nothing to do with you at all. A spirited eight-year-old who cannot get a math problem to come out right may fly off the handle with no provocation from a parent.

Whether or not the tantrum is part of a power struggle with you, the child will still be aware of how you respond to his tantrum. As the late psychologist Rudolf Dreikurs once observed, people do not *lose* their temper, they *use* their temper. Your child's show of anger is bringing about some desired payoff.

This payoff may be internal: the "letting off steam" phenomenon that may help reduce the chemical buildup that has resulted from intense frustration. Although these hurricanelike expressions of anger eventually blow themselves out, they often do damage to people, property, and relationships in their way. Plus, the spirited child at the eye of the storm is in turmoil. Parents understandably want to do something to intervene, but what they do can make future tantrums either more or less likely.

When you either fight or give in during a tantrum, you may inadvertently create a secondary, external payoff that produces more tantrums down the road. When you get angry and fight with your child during a tantrum, you give her power over your emotions, a major payoff to a powerful child or teen. When you give in to unreasonable demands or overprotect and pamper her in an attempt to solve the problem, you also create a payoff that makes future tantrums likely.

Your best bet is to stay calm, cool, and collected. Either offer help in cooling down your child or take your sails out of his wind for a brief period of time so that he does not have an audience to perform for.

1. When the child has a tantrum, for whatever reason, say something like, "You are overheated. Let's cool down first, then we can work on a solution."

2. Ask your child: "Would you like some help cooling down, or would you like to cool down on your own?"

3. If he continues crying, either say: "OK, I'll let you have some time alone to cool down. Let me know when you are back in control, and we'll talk about the problem some more." Then give him some space, but stay close by. Or, go straight to step 5.

4-A. If he follows you, say, "I guess you want some help cooling off. Let's take some deep breaths together."

4-B. If he doesn't follow you and cools down, go back in and say, "You did a good job cooling yourself down. What did you do that worked?"

5. If he continues crying, come back in five to ten minutes and say, "You are really overheated. It looks like you could use some help cooling off this time. Let's take some deep breaths together." If he screams louder and gets angrier, say, "OK, I guess you don't want my help right now. Let me know if you do." Then leave and come back again in five minutes to offer again, "Are you ready to cool off and talk about the problem? What can I do to help you cool off?" Suggest things that have worked in the past. For example:

- "How about a hug?"
- "A glass of water?"
- "Some deep breathing?"
- "Could you use a bath?"
- "Can you think of something else that might work?"
- "What else could you do?"
- "Do you want to hit the pillow some?" (Using a pillow for a

punching bag is a good way for some kids to express their anger nondestructively.)

- "How about some time in your special cool place?"

Another strategy that sometimes works is to find a way to engage the child's cerebral cortex—his thinking brain. During a tantrum, all of the brain energy has been rustled to the brain's emotional centers. Finding a way to "trick" the energy back to the rational brain can reset the balance. This technique is a bit risky and can easily backfire, getting your child even angrier, so be on guard and back off if you see negative results. However, it does work sometimes, and asking your child a question that requires some thought is one way to do this. For example: "I know you are angry right now.

- "Let's try counting slowly to ten." (Or counting slowly to twenty by twos.)

Or . . .

- "Do you remember what we are planning to do this weekend?"
- "How many days before Saturday?"

Or . . .

- "If your anger were fire, how hot would it be right now?"
- "If you could put a big cube of ice on that fire to cool you down, how big an ice cube would you need?"

Or . . .

- "What color is your stove right now?"
- "How hot is your thermometer right now?"
- Can you make it just a little bit cooler?

Some kids can also be jostled out of their emotional state with humor. Others will become even more upset by your attempts to be funny and consider it disrespectful, so be careful. If they respond with more anger, apologize and back off.

For younger kids, you might try buying a stuffed animal or a funny-sounding animal and hiding it somewhere in the house. Then, when your child has a tantrum, ask, "I know you are upset right now, but maybe it would help if you could tell me where the unicorn is hiding? Could you help me look for him?" If he bites, then the two of you can go on a unicorn hunt, and it will be impossible for him to stay angry. Then the next time he gets angry, you have a new metaphor for helping him cool down: "Boy, you are really having a hard time cooling down. Maybe we need to go on another unicorn hunt. What do you think? I wonder where he is hiding this time?"

For an older child, you might try turning his anger into a humorous compliment. For example, "You know, if you could harness the energy that you are expending right now, I bet you could throw a baseball one hundred miles an hour." Or try a straight compliment: "I know you are feeling really angry right now, but I have to admire the amount of determination you have."

Notice that through all of these suggestions, you are neither fighting nor giving in. Your role is that of a concerned helper who wants to see her child learn to self-soothe to cool himself down when he gets emotionally overheated, and to solve problems and handle frustrations effectively. But what if nothing works? Sometimes a spirited child is so caught up in his emotions that nothing you do or say will calm him down. This is why prevention is so important. However, when he is over the top, and you cannot find a way to help, you may have to say gently, "Well, nothing I can do seems to be helping, but I know you will cool down when you ready. Let me know when you want to talk." Make sure that he is in a safe place, then leave the room or go about your own business, giving him little attention. Sometimes all we can do is to remove ourselves as an audience and let kids calm down on their own.

"What Have You Learned?"

What you and your child learn from handling a power struggle or episode of intense anger will help determine how soon another one occurs. By refusing to fight or give in, even if you are unable to help cool your child down, you will have taught him that his anger does not get a major payoff. You can add to the learning by making a few simple rules and consequences clear:

- "It is OK to get angry, even very angry, but how you choose to express your anger can be either OK or not OK. For example, it is not OK to be destructive, disrespectful, or violent against another person. But hitting a pillow, box, or punching bag is OK."

If your child breaks any of these rules, talk to her after she cools down about the importance of the rule. Then make sure that she understands that she will need to accept a logical consequence for doing so. For example:

- Being destructive: She must use her allowance to help pay for any damage. (You can help pay if it is too expensive, but she should feel the sting of losing money to offset damage.)

- Being disrespectful: He loses out on something connected to the disrespect. For example, if he had a tantrum over not being allowed to stay out late and called you names, he might lose the privilege of going out at all for a week.

- Being violent against people. With the zero-tolerance policy in schools these days, you need to be very firm about not allowing kids to hit, bite, or otherwise attack others, including yourself. For younger kids, removing him from others when he does so is an effective consequence. Just pick him up and say, "We don't hit [bite, slap, spit at, or kick] other people. You can come back when you can be around others without hitting." Then take him to his room or other time-out area.

- With older kids, prevent them from hurting anyone at the time and ask them to leave the room. After they have calmed down, talk about what they did and why it is not OK. Then ask them to help come up with a logical consequence. It should include making it up to the attacked person in some way. It could be staying home that weekend and writing a letter of apology or something else that makes sense to you both.

In addition to logical consequences, take time to talk with your child about what worked and what didn't work for reducing the anger. Ask questions such as:

- "When you got to your boiling point yesterday, do you remember what you were thinking that pushed you over the edge?"
- "When your stove got red hot, what did it feel like to you?"
- "How did you finally calm yourself down?"
- "Was there anything that I did that helped or hurt?"
- "What would you like for me to do the same or differently next time?"

Your goal is not to hurt your child's feelings and punish her beyond the logical consequences that you have set up but to be an ally who wants to help her solve her anger problem in a beneficial way. If you have let your own temper get the best of you, too, be sure to acknowledge that fact and, if appropriate, apologize and try to make it up to your child. Above all, when anger has come between you, it is important to reestablish a connection that says "We still love each other, value each other, and want the best for each other." A good hug, some fun time, or even quiet time together, and a heartfelt "I love you" could be just what the doctor ordered.

11

"Palms Up," Pardner

It has long been thought that the key to empathy is the mother-child connection—that if a mother is loving and nurturing, the child will learn by her compassionate example. But new studies suggest that it is the involvement of the father that is the most important variable in the development of empathy in children—in particular, his ability to be both warm and to set limits on unacceptable behavior.

—Victoria Secunda,
American psychologist and
author, *Women and Their
Fathers* (1992)

OLD-SCHOOL PARENTING HAD the father as the disciplinarian and the mother as the nurturer in parent-child relations. "Wait till your father comes home!" became the battle cry of the defeated mother and "Better talk to your mother about that" the hollow words of the baffled, tough-guy dad. But as mothers began realizing that they were giving away their power, and men began realizing that they were giving away their hearts, the two roles have gradually merged. Today's active parents recognize the need to be both nurturing and firm with their children, and to develop the skills and attitudes for doing so. Spirited children in particular need parents who have the backbone to set limits with them as well as the empathy to comfort and support them in solving problems.

We have focused a good deal of attention in this book on how to set limits, and in doing so, I have stressed the need to be aware of your child's feelings and desires so that you reduce the likelihood of a power struggle. The FLAC method (feelings, limits, alternatives, and consequences) combines many of these responses in a single discipline method. I have also described times when your spirited child simply needs a firm reminder without all the fuss. "Harold, throwing food is not allowed." "Cynthia, you may not run in the house." "Tonya, clean up this mess now."

Setting firm limits using any of the discipline skills presented earlier will help your child learn that he lives in a community with others who have needs and rights just as important as his own. Without this knowledge, your child will likely become (or remain) a self-centered brat who thinks the world revolves around her and her desires. Rude and obnoxious behavior is not only a pain to others but often leads to breaking rules and laws. This lands your child in big trouble at school and perhaps with the law. In fact, prisons are filled with spirited adults who never learned to consider the needs of others as well as themselves and who never experienced consistent discipline at home.

But discipline is not enough to teach your child real empathy for others or how to solve problems cooperatively when others are involved. I suggest that these two abilities—empathy and cooperative problem solving—are not only important in keeping your child out of trouble but are essential for real success in the world at large. So, coupled with your willingness and ability to provide clear, firm limits to misbehavior, you may also want to strengthen your skills in teaching problem solving and empathy. If so, you have come to the right chapter.

The Parable of the Roman Galley

There was once a Roman galley where each of the slaves rowed to the beat of the drum. One slave looked over at the slave next to him and noticed that the second slave was drilling a hole under his seat. As water began gushing into the galley, the first slave exclaimed in horror, "What in Jupiter's name are you doing?!" "What's it to you?" replied the second slave as he continued to drill. "I'm only drilling the hole under *my* seat."

What makes this story humorous is our knowledge that no matter whose seat the hole is drilled under, when we are all riding in the same boat, it affects us all. The total lack of empathy that the hole driller showed for his fellow slaves demonstrates an exaggerated failure to understand how his behavior affects others around him. Spirited children are often in this boat. They can be so focused on their own wants and needs that they fail to realize how their behavior comes across and impacts others. Teaching them empathy—the ability to put themselves in the shoes of others and feel what someone else feels—is essential if we want them to stay safe and dry.

Empathy Does It

Teaching your child to feel for others begins with helping him learn to identify his own feelings. The tendency for most parents of spirited children is to become consumed with behavior—or more specifically, misbehavior. While this is essential in teaching kids what is off-limits and how to behave well, it does not really help them understand others and how their misbehavior affects others.

Begin by asking yourself what your child is feeling in any given situation. Does he seem happy, sad, angry, joyous, nervous, hurt, excited, or anything else? Once you have a found a word that seems to catch his feeling, try feeling that emotion yourself. In other words, try empathizing with your child. Once you have it, reflect the word back to him both verbally and with a corresponding facial expression and tone of voice. For example:

"You seem happy, Phillip." (You smile, and your voice is upbeat to indicate happiness.)

"You seem kind of sad, Erica." (Your face and voice show concern.)

"Wow, you really sound angry, Thomas." (Your brow narrows a little as if angry, and your voice sounds strong.)

"You are one joyous kid today, aren't you Felice?" (Your face and voice are joyous.)

"That really hurt, didn't it, John?" (Again, your face shows concern, as your voice lowers and also indicates your concern.)

Notice that you are using tentative phrases and not absolutes. "You seem," "You sound," "Didn't it?" Such phrases let your child know that you are not pretending to be a mind reader but are trying to get a handle on what she is feeling. If you are correct in your guess, an amazing thing happens. Your child's head will nod up and down in agreement, and she will continue talking. This phenomenon is sometimes known as "feeling felt," and it has been linked in recent research to healthy brain growth and development. Kids who feel felt by their parents know that they have an ally to help them through the tough times and to share in their happiness during the good times. This goes to our basic human need to feel a sense of belonging, of connectedness with others, and no one is more important to a child to connect with than his parents.

What if your feeling words miss the mark? As long as you have stated it in a tentative form, your child can easily correct you, and no harm is done. For example:

PARENT: "You seem happy, Phillip."

CHILD: "I'm not really happy—just relieved."

PARENT: "Oh, I see. You are relieved to have it over with."

CHILD: "Yeah. I thought that week would last forever!"

PARENT: "I know what you mean. I've had weeks like that, too."

By using the tentative "you seem," this parent was easily able to shift feeling words from happy to relieved when her child corrected her guess. She then further joined her child by saying "I know what you mean. I've had weeks like that." The idea of joining your child emotionally is at the heart of empathy. Let yourself feel her joy, sadness, anger, disgust, or any emotion. Do not worry about whether the emotion is "right or wrong" or if it is based on rational or irrational thinking at this point. Just determine what the feeling is and reflect that feeling back to your child. If he is angry that he missed his favorite TV show, don't minimize it by saying "That's OK, there are always more shows." Instead, empathize with him by saying something like:

- "It's really disappointing when you miss something you were looking forward to, isn't it?"
- "I'm sorry. I know how much you enjoy that show."
- "Awww, I hate when that happens, too."

Later we will discuss how to solve the problem, but the first step is to establish empathy, that feeling of feeling felt. When your child knows that he can count on you for that, he will be much more inclined to open up and share his concerns, problems, hopes, and even dreams with you.

Avoiding Sidewinders

In the Mojave and Sonoran deserts of the southwestern United States lives a rattlesnake known as a Sidewinder. This venomous snake gets its name from the fact that it does not approach its prey head-on like most snakes but moves at a diagonal angle through the sand. In tales of the Old West, the name *sidewinder* came to represent a type of person who could not be trusted, as he moved in duplicitous and disingenuous ways. In old Western movies, many a gunfight scene began with the words "Hold it right there, sidewinder!"

In order to respond to your child's feeling as a first step in teaching her empathy and respect for others' feelings, you have to avoid some common pitfalls. I'll call these pitfalls sidewinders for two reasons. First, they do not deal with your child's emotions head-on but try to come at them from some more comfortable angle. And two, these sidewinders can kill the communication with your child faster than the strike of a rattlesnake. Let's take a look at some of the more common communication sidewinders and how the child often hears the message. As an example, let's say that your child is having trouble putting together a puzzle and is getting very frustrated. You are afraid he will lose control entirely and have a major tantrum. Your fear outweighs your empathy, and so you resort to a sidewinder tactic, such as:

COMMANDING: "Put this piece in here."
WHAT THE CHILD HEARS: "You are too dumb to work this out for yourself."
BLAMING: "If you would slow down like I told you, it wouldn't be so difficult."
WHAT THE CHILD HEARS: "You never do anything right."
INTERROGATING: "Why did you start a puzzle that was too hard for you?"
WHAT THE CHILD HEARS: "I'm not good enough, and she knows it."
MINIMIZING: "Come on, it's only a puzzle. Don't get so excited."
WHAT THE CHILD HEARS: "My feelings don't matter."
BELITTLING: "You know you aren't very good at puzzles. Why are you even trying?"
WHAT THE CHILD HEARS: "I'm a loser."
PSYCHOLOGIZING: "Are you trying to have a tantrum with this?"
WHAT THE CHILD HEARS: "She thinks I'm devious."

EXAGGERATING: "If you can't do a simple puzzle, what chance do you
        have to do well in school this year?"
WHAT THE CHILD HEARS: "I'm worse off than I imagined."
BEING A KNOW-IT-ALL: "If you had asked me for some help, you
        wouldn't have had this problem to begin with."
WHAT THE CHILD HEARS: "I'll never be able to do things for myself."
PLACATING: "You're so good at other things, I wouldn't worry too much
        about a silly puzzle."
WHAT THE CHILD HEARS: "My concerns don't matter."
MORALIZING: "You really shouldn't let things get you so upset."
WHAT THE CHILD HEARS: "There is something wrong with me."
NEGATIVE humor: "I guess you have a case of PDD—Puzzle Deficit
        Disorder (ha-ha-ha)."
WHAT THE CHILD HEARS: "I'm a big joke around here."
BEING SARCASTIC: "Well, genius, I guess puzzles just aren't your thing."
WHAT THE CHILD HEARS: "I'm dumb, and you're mean!"

While admittedly some of these sidewinders are worse than others, they all share the common characteristic of ignoring the child's feeling. When parents use them, the intent is usually to help solve a problem, not make it worse. But the way the child hears the message involves not feeling felt, not feeling cared about, and not feeling good enough. The discouragement that is triggered usually leads to the problem getting worse or other problems springing up in their place. Instead, the best first step is to take a deep breath and respond to the child's feeling. For example:

"Puzzles can sure be frustrating sometimes." Or:
"You seem to be getting pretty frustrated over there." And maybe add:
"Is your stove heating up?" (Or whatever metaphor you and your child have
        established to measure increases in frustration and anger.)

Your voice and facial expression should communicate concern, because, after all, if you are really empathizing with your child, you will feel some of his frustration along with him. Then once you have connected with your child at a feeling level, and she feels your concern, move on to problem solving.

Palms-Up Problem Solving

There are basically two types of problems that parents face with their children: problems of discipline and problems of support. Problems of discipline occur when your child tests the limits by breaking a family rule or otherwise misbehaving. These are the times to use the discipline skills presented in chapters 6 through 8. The problems that we are addressing in this chapter are problems that belong to your child—problems that he has a right to solve for himself. A frustrating puzzle, a conflict with a friend, the fact that it rained, and you can't go to the zoo as planned. These and a thousand other child-owned problems can send a spirited child into a tailspin that ends in hours of suffering for everyone around. While it is tempting to jump in and provide a quick fix to such problems, doing so does nothing to teach your child the essential skill of problem solving. In such cases, your job is to offer support and guide your child toward coming up with a solution for himself.

I call this "palms-up" problem solving, to contrast it with the finger pointing that often accompanies the words "Here's what you need to do." Instead of taking over, you actually turn the palms of your hands upward and say something to the effect of "I don't know what you will decide to do, but let's look at your choices." This simple gesture and message says to the child:

1. "I'm not here to take over and run your life." This is important to the power motive of a spirited child, because if he suspects that you are trying to run his life, he will rebel all the harder.

2. "My hands are empty. I'm not holding a weapon." The non-verbal act of turning palms up actually led to the custom of hand shaking; again, a sign of not holding a weapon, or (now taken metaphorically) a sign that the other person is in no danger from you and may very well have an ally.

3. Asking your child to look at his choices with you says that he does have an ally, and he also has potential solutions to his problem. Both of these messages are encouraging and can motivate the child to work out a solution.

4. The thought processes required to look at options engage the thinking brain and pull energy away from the more primitive emotional areas. This serves to reduce his frustration and anger and return his brain to calmer functioning. Going back to our example of the frustrating puzzle, the dialogue might go like this:

PARENT: "Puzzles can sure be frustrating sometimes."

CHILD: "It's stupid!"

PARENT: "You sound pretty angry. Is your stove heating up?"

CHILD: [*No response.*]

PARENT: "I bet it's starting to get red. What do you think?"

CHILD: "I hate this puzzle!"

PARENT: [*Turning palms up.*] Well, I don't know what you will decide to do, but let's look at your choices. What do you think you could do to cool your stove down a little?

So far the parent has done two things to help her child solve his problem:

1. She empathized with him emotionally, using the feeling word *frustrating* while indicating her concern with her voice tone and facial expression.

2. She used the palms-up gesture to transition into looking at possible solutions to his problem.

3. Her third step will be to help him evaluate his options by considering possible consequences and then trying one. This step involves some synergistic problem solving, where one person's suggestion may fuel an idea in the other person until a viable solution emerges. This process works well in creative corporations, and it works at home with spirited children. It is important that no ideas are put down. But because spirited children often focus just on the here and now, it is up to the parent to help them think about the possible future consequences of their choices. Questions like the following can help you do just that:

- "What could you do?"
- "What might happen if you did that?"
- "What else could you do?"
- "What do you think would happen if you . . ." (Introduce your own suggestion here, but do not try to force or cajole your child into accepting it. This is his problem, and he has to make the decision. Remember, kids often learn from their mistakes as well as their successes, so do not be afraid to let him try something that you are pretty sure will fail—unless, of course, it involves health, safety, or your family values. In those cases, just remind him that this option is outside the limits, giving him the reason why. Then move on to other choices.)

Let's continue with our dialogue example:

PARENT: [*Turning palms up* . . .] "Well, I don't know what you will decide to do, but let's look at your choices. What do you think you could do to cool your stove down a little?"

CHILD: "I could tear this stupid puzzle into a million pieces!"

PARENT: [*Laughing*] That would probably feel pretty good right now, but then you wouldn't have the puzzle later."

CHILD: "That's the idea!"

PARENT: [*Smiling at his joke*] "Well, it's your puzzle, so if you want to get rid of it, I guess you can. But maybe we should give it away to a needy organization so other kids can play with it."

CHILD: "I don't really want to get rid of it. It's just really hard."

PARENT: "Well, what else can you do to calm down?"

CHILD: "I guess I could take a break and come back later."

PARENT: "That usually helps you keep your cool. Why don't we get something to drink and then take a look at the puzzle together? I know a few tricks about puzzles that might help."

Once you have helped your child look at some options, evaluate possible consequences, and make a choice, the ball is in his court. Give him a chance to put his choice into action. Or, if you are involved—as in the above example—help him put his plan into action. Then once he has had a chance to try his solution, be sure to go on to the fourth step.

4. Follow up to see how his solution is working. If you are not around when he tries his solution, make a point to ask him how it went. If it went well, offer some encouragement. If it did not work out, go back to step one and offer empathy, followed by steps two and three. You can simply continue problem solving together until another possible solution is agreed upon. This process will eventually build a cooperative relationship, as it teaches your child how to find solutions to his problems, including the problem of anger. Again, the four steps to palms-up problem solving are:

1. Empathy: Reflect the child's feelings with words, tone, and facial expression.

2. Brainstorming: Turn palms up and brainstorm possible solutions.

3. Action: Assist in predicting consequences and then making a choice to put into action.

4. Follow up: Check in later to see how it went and continue the process if necessary.

Teaching Respect and Empathy for Others

Responding to your child's feelings with concern and empathy not only helps you help her with problems, it also models how to show concern and empathy for others. This is an important characteristic of successful people in our society. Unfortunately, it does not come easily to spirited children. This is partly a function of their CAPPS nature, as being more curious, adventurous, powerful, persistent, and sensitive conspire to make them more self-centered. It is also sometimes a function of parenting that allows too much freedom to spirited children to impose their will on others.

For example, while recently staying in a hotel that offered free breakfast to its guests, I got into a conversation with the lady in charge of the dining area. I joked that serving good food for free was a great formula for attracting a lot of customers. She said she didn't mind a full house made up of adults, but the kids could be a real problem. I asked her what she meant, and she told me that too many parents just let their kids do whatever they wanted in the dining room.

"The other day," she informed me, "one kid poured syrup in my waffle iron and then just flat-out denied doing it. His parents didn't do a thing." Spirited kids or not, too many parents allow their children to create problems for others to handle. This is not only unfair to others, it does a disservice to the children who need to learn to respect the rights and feelings of others in order to get along in this world.

Providing respectful discipline is the first step, but then addressing the values of respect and empathy is a strong second.

Spirited children tend to see everything through their own eyes. You can help them learn to value respect and concern for others by making *statements* like these:

- "Everybody has the right to be treated respectfully."
- "I don't talk to you like that, and I don't expect you to talk to me like that."
- "People need to know that others care about how they feel."
- "When you feel bad, you want others to care. Well, others are the same way. They want to know that you care."
- "She must have felt very hurt when that happened."
- "I bet that really made her angry."
- "That makes me feel great. Thanks!"
- "You have a good heart."
- "I like the way that you showed concern for your brother."
- "That was very respectful. Thank you."
- "What a generous thing to do!"

You can also help expand their sensitivity to others by asking *questions* like these:

- "What do you think she was feeling right then?"
- "How would you have felt if you were in her shoes?"
- "What do you think that I am feeling right now?"
- "What would you have felt like if someone had done that to you?"
- "What could you do to make him feel better?"
- "Do you think she was being respectful when she said that?"
- "Was that a respectful thing to do?"
- "How could you let her know that you care about her feelings?"

Establishing ties means seeing your child at a feeling level, well beyond the behavior and misbehavior that characterize so much of parent-child relationships: learning to listen for your child's inner voice that tells about his fears and hurts that lie beneath the sound and fury of his anger; picking up on the bits of pride she feels as she masters a difficult task or learns to manage her temper. These feelings aren't available to the normal senses of sight and sound. They require you to listen with that part of your parental intuition called heart. Learn to listen to your child heart to heart and then respond with knowledge and empathy and you will reach her at a level that creates the tie that tames.

12

Using Outside Resources: Calling in the Cavalry

The race of man would surely perish did they cease to aid each
other. We cannot exist without mutual help. All therefore that need
aid have a right to ask it from their fellow-men; and no one who
has the power of granting can refuse it without guilt.

—SIR WALTER SCOTT (1771–
1832), Scottish novelist and poet

We will surely get to our destination if we join hands.

—AUNG SAN SUU KYI (1945–),
Burmese political leader

IF YOU DO everything in this book except what I am going to recommend in this chapter, my guess is that you will probably fail in
your attempt to tame your spirited child. Put another way, if you
do what I am going to recommend in this chapter, you will increase
your chances of success exponentially. There are at least three good
reasons for this. First, spirited children have so much energy that
if you go it alone, they will most likely wear you out before you
manage to tame them. For such kids, sending in the cavalry is not
just an option, it is a necessity. And by *cavalry,* I mean any of a
number of useful outside resources that can help you achieve your
goal of taming your spirited child. You do not need to use all of
these resources, but you had better use some. And by *some,* I mean
more than one.

The second reason that using outside resources is so helpful is that learning often requires repetition. When your child hears the same positive messages over and over from different people in different settings, the message has a better chance of getting through. Of course, this means choosing outside resources that share your values and goals for your child. If you believe in the philosophy of this book, that means finding resources that want to teach your child to live within the limits of responsible behavior without breaking his spirit or will; resources that will help you build on the positive aspects of his spirited traits and use his CAPPS (curiosity, adventurousness, power, persistence, and sensitivity) in useful ways.

Finally, it is worth keeping in mind that no child gets everything he needs from his parents. All children, and especially spirited children, need the lessons they can learn from other well-intentioned and capable adults to supplement what they learn at home (and, in some cases, to actually replace it). Wise parents will tap these resources and nurture such positive relationships and opportunities for their child. I'll cover the following resources in this chapter, but keep an eye out for others as well. Then use your best judgment about how and where to use them:

- The school
- Spiritual education
- Mental health resources
- Sports, arts, hobbies, and recreation
- Friends and relatives

The School

When our son, Ben, was four years old and at his most spirited, we found a terrific ally in the teachers and administrators of his school. His kindergarten teacher, a kind and experienced woman who could dish out both encouragement and firmness in equal measure as the children needed, was very willing to work with us in teaching Ben that group living required accepting rules and limits on his freedom. She also recognized that spark of life that was uniquely his and found ways to nurture that as well. Within the course of that year, his tantrums disappeared, and the beginning of the mature and cooperative young man that he is today began to emerge.

When I speak to groups of teachers, I show them a cartoon that depicts two men meeting each other on parents' night at a school. They are both disheveled to the point of looking like they have been through the ringer. One of the men offers his hand to the other and says, "You must be Timmy's teacher. I'm Timmy's father." The joke, of course, is that both have experienced Timmy's spirit in ways that make them natural allies. Taming Timmy is in both their interests, as well as in Timmy's. But too often parents and teachers offend each other and turn a powerful natural alliance into a power struggle between adversaries. The following tips can help you build a cooperative relationship with your child's teacher and others at the school:

- First, get your child into the best school you can afford. If that means moving to a neighborhood with better schools, move. What makes a better school? Part of it is the quality of the staff. A concerned teacher who goes beyond the curriculum and takes a personal interest in students can make for a life-changing experience. An even bigger factor, however, according to more than a hundred studies, is the involvement of the parents at the school. Kids at schools with high parent involvement do better in everything from academics to behavior. Children of such parents tend to be more motivated to do well in school and to behave more appropriately. This creates positive peer pressure on children to do good work and behave respectfully. That is a hard combination to beat, and one that is difficult to overcome when missing.

- Be an involved parent wherever your child goes to school. This includes everything from showing up at school events to volunteering to making sure schoolwork and positive behavior are priorities with your child. There are plenty of good books on how to do this effectively.

- Recognize that teachers, administrators, and others have feelings, too. They may be in powerful positions, but like all of us, they thrive on encouragement, support, and approval and become defensive when attacked or criticized. This does not mean that you should never confront a teacher but that you go in with your palms up—not your dukes up.

- Give the staff the benefit of the doubt. Most teachers and administrators are capable and concerned educators. Start with the assumption that yours is and that with a positive approach from you, you can bring that part out even more.

- Be honest with yourself. Yes, your spirited child is wonderful, but she can also be a handful. Do not be ashamed or try to hide that fact. Together you and the school can help her build on the wonderful part.

- Support the school's discipline plan. When your child gets in trouble at school, he should also know that he is in trouble at home. Explain to him why his behavior was out of line and how he can better handle such situations in the future. If appropriate, add a logical consequence at home to help reinforce the message. For example, when

Kyle talked back to his teacher, his mother explained the importance of speaking respectfully to others, especially those in charge, and had him spend the day writing a letter of apology to his teacher.

- Ask for a conference with the teacher as early in the year as possible. Explain the situation and ask for her help in working together to teach your child how to live cooperatively. Discuss how you will communicate, so that each of you will know what is going on at home and at school. Then stay in touch throughout the year, being sure to find opportunities to offer mutual encouragement and support.

A Spirited Child's Spiritual Education

A good religious affiliation can be a godsend to parents attempting to tame a spirited child. Humans have been spiritual beings since the first man or woman looked up into the heavens and wondered where we came from and what our purpose in living was going to be. As we evolved, our conception of spirituality evolved with us, and today there are hundreds of different approaches to these questions. The commonality is that all of them share the belief that there is a higher power in the universe than humans. This belief can be both humbling and empowering, depending on how it is interpreted. As the Jewish Talmud suggests, people would do well to keep two pieces of paper, one in each pocket, to be read when needed. On one is to be written "For me, God made all of this!" On the other, "I am nothing but dust." Humility and empowerment, two sides of the same spiritual coin, seem to be needed by humans at different times.

Your spirited child will probably benefit tremendously from a loving spiritual education. When I say "loving," I am creating a caveat that excludes those religious organizations that teach fear and even hatred of those who do not share their spiritual beliefs. Such groups will likely tap into the natural power drive of spirited children and use that in destructive ways. I also caution against those organizations that use old-school dictatorial approaches with children in order to control their behavior and keep them subservient. These methods are likely to produce power struggles and/or create a negative reaction in the child toward spirituality in general.

One final caveat: If you and your spouse are confirmed atheists, then sending your child off for a spiritual education that is based on a belief in God may create a rift between you and your child that undermines the gains that such an education might otherwise produce. You may be better off looking toward building a spiritual base through communion with nature, caring for others, or in other ways that make sense to you—and do so as a family unit or with others who share similar beliefs.

The positive effects of a loving spiritual education can be profound for spirited children. I've found over the years that a strong, positive youth group based on spiritual values can be especially helpful in turning around spirited children who were already in serious trouble. Successful programs approach children where they are—with fun activities, engaging stories, and group camaraderie rather than with heavy-handed theological tactics. They often stress the basic worth of the child and build a sense of self-esteem and value. These programs also have the benefit of peer leadership through older kids and young adults who have an easier time reaching children, given the way that kids tend to look up to older peers. When thinking about a spiritual education for your child, consider the following:

- Most major religions teach a version of the Golden Rule: "Do unto others as you would have others do unto you." From this amazing concept, your child will learn other lessons that you will also be teaching at home, including responsibility, respect, empathy, cooperation, courage, humility, justice, love, and more.

- If you are not actively involved with a religious organization yourself, but once were or are open to the experience, this is a great time to make the effort. Try out a number of settings and see what feels right to you (and your partner if you have one). You may find that there is a lot of positive opportunity for you as well as your child.

- If one parent wants to participate on a regular basis and the other doesn't, this is OK. Your child can still get a tremendous amount out of the experience, as long as the parents are respectful of each other's beliefs or lack of belief.

- Caution: If you make religion a power struggle between the adults, then your child will likely feel the fallout, and much will be lost. Again, mutual respect for the opinions of others, as long as those opinions are not harmful, is an important part of family life, as it is of a loving spiritual life as well.

- Work with your child's Sunday school teacher in much the same way that you work with his academic teacher. Your support and encouragement are important, and you may find that the religious instructor is willing to go beyond the call of duty in helping your child. Years ago, as a young Sunday school teacher myself while I was still in graduate school, I made home visits to help the parents of a particularly spirited student. This was long before the TV shows *Supernanny* and *Nanny 911* were in vogue, but the boy's parents truly appreciated my personal interest in their son.

Mental Health Resources

While there is no medication for spirited children per se, and while therapeutic treatment is not usually required to tame a spirited child, many such children have other problems that are separate from their spirited nature. These problems can often be helped with therapy (with or without medication). The recommendations made in this book are still valid and should accompany other treatment, but, for example, if your child is both spirited and has ADHD (attention deficit/hyperactivity disorder), he will benefit from services aimed at treating his ADHD as well as what you are doing to tame him. This may include medication, counseling, and other interventions.

It is beyond the scope of this book to describe all of the childhood problems that currently exist; there are other books that go into this in more detail. However, take a look at the following list of common problems. If some of the symptoms seem to describe your child, either find a book or other resource on the problem to understand it more thoroughly and/or take your child to a professional to have him evaluated. With each of these problems, the difference between what is considered normal and what often requires treatment has to do with the degree of symptoms and how much the problem is interfering with the child's and family's lives.

- **Anxiety disorders.** These disorders are characterized by excessive worry, fear, or uneasiness and may occur in as many as 13 percent of children and teens. They include phobias, panic disorders, obsessive-compulsive disorder, post-traumatic stress disorder, and generalized anxiety disorder.

- **Mood disorders.** This includes severe depression as well as bipolar disorder, in which children experience severe mood swings that range from extreme highs to deep depression.

- **Attention deficit/hyperactivity disorder.** Children with ADHD have trouble focusing their attention and are often impulsive and easily distracted. They have great difficulty sitting still, taking turns, and keeping quiet.

- **Learning disorders.** These disorders affect children of normal or above-average intelligence in ways that make it difficult for them to learn. Learning disorders can show up as problems with written and spoken language, mathematics, coordination, attention, or self-control.

- **Eating, sleeping, and toileting problems.** This category includes children (more often teenagers) who are intensely afraid of gaining weight although they are in fact underweight (anorexia) and those who binge on food and then rid their bodies of the food by vomiting, abusing laxatives, taking enemas, or exercising excessively (bulimia). Sleeping disorders include kids who have trouble sleeping, sleep too much, are up at night and sleep during the day, and those who fall asleep involuntarily during the day (narcolepsy). Toilet problems include encopresis, which is a tendency for a child above the age of four to defecate in inappropriate places, and enuresis, which is the tendency of a child above the age of five to urinate in inappropriate places either during the day or night. With any of these problems, occasional accidents are not signs of a disorder.

- **Autism and Asperger syndrome.** These are disorders in which the child has difficulty communicating with others. Autism, which is the more severe of the two, may include repetition of behaviors over time such as head banging, rocking, or spinning objects. A milder form of this disorder, Asperger syndrome, is characterized by poor social skills and habitual inappropriate behavior.

- **Schizophrenia.** This disorder is characterized by psychotic periods in which the child may experience hallucinations, extreme withdrawal, and loss of contact with reality.

- **Conduct disorder.** These kids have little concern for others and often violate the rules of society. They tend to act out their feelings and impulses in destructive ways, often landing them in trouble with authority. Offenses may include lying, theft, aggression, truancy, setting fires, and vandalism. If not treated, offenses usually grow more severe over time as the individual gets into more and more trouble with authority and eventually the law. Spirited children do not rise to the level of conduct disorder, although if not tamed, they may eventually escalate into this category.

Three Levels of Intervention

With any problem of childhood, there are three general levels of help. These interventions progress from the least invasive to the most, so it is generally wise to proceed from one to the next as necessary. The exception occurs when a child is in an emergency situation such as a suicide attempt or drug overdose. These three levels of intervention are:

1. **Parenting education.** Developing your own knowledge and skills in order to help your child is the first step that most parents take in order to help their spirited child. This may be as informal as talking to a friend or physician, reading a book, or enrolling in a multisession parent education course. All can be very valuable, but a good parenting course has the added advantage of reinforcing skills over time with the aid of an experienced group leader, the support of other parents, and the backbone of an effective curriculum. The hours spent in such programs have truly changed

the lives of millions of children and their families for the better. You can find one through your child's school or pediatrician, religious institutions or mental health organizations, or check the reference section of this book.

Related to parent education are the various parent support groups formed around many disorders. For example, CHADD (Children and Adults with Attention Deficit Disorders) groups are available throughout the U.S. and other countries, and have offered support and information to many people dealing with this problem. Check the internet for organizations that support problems that your family is experiencing.

2. **Individual or family therapy.** When parent education is not enough to bring about the change that is needed, the next logical step is to seek out the services of a capable mental health professional. This might be a counselor, social worker, psychologist, psychiatrist, or another of the so-called "helping professionals" who are trained to work with child-centered problems. Some of these therapists will choose to work with the entire family, while others prefer to spend most of their time working with the child or even the parents. I would avoid any therapist who wants to see *only* the child and has no concrete suggestions for what you might do at home. After all, he or she will be with the child only an hour or two a week, while you will be with him for much of the other 167 hours. It makes sense for the therapist to work with you as a team to bring about the desired change in your child.

You should be aware that a therapist's ability to help you is not necessarily related to her degree. There are brilliant masters-level therapists, and there are those who leave a lot to be desired. This is true of therapists at all levels. However, only psychiatrists have an MD degree and so are the only therapists who are licensed to prescribe medication. Psychiatrists are usually the most expensive therapists as well. So if your child may benefit from medication, make sure that your therapist is either a psychiatrist or works with one for medication purposes. Many mental health clinics are set up this way, so that clients see less-expensive therapists for weekly sessions and a psychiatrist to regulate medication treatment.

There is a very real concern in our society that children are overly medicated. Some parents feel that they should never put a child on medication, while others run to their pediatrician shouting "Ritalin, Ritalin!" at the first sign of distractibility. As with most controversies, there is usually some truth to both positions. I believe that too many children are medicated in our society, when other approaches would be more effective with less risk. On the other hand, many children derive tremendous benefit from a carefully controlled drug regimen and would never achieve such positive results without them. The key is to work with a qualified and capable therapist to evaluate medication as one component of treatment. Never think that medication alone is all that is needed. Even when medication is called for, the research indicates that the best results occur with a combination of medication and therapy.

There are a number of good ways to find a therapist or a therapeutic team. First, check your health insurance and see what coverage is provided and what limitations are in effect. A personal recommendation from a friend who has had a good experience with a therapist is often a good source. Your child's pediatrician is a good resource for helping you assess the problem and referring you to a therapist for further evaluation and/or treatment. Your local community mental health center can be found in the yellow pages and can usually offer affordable treatment. Your child's school counselor or psychologist (with whom you have already been working, hopefully) is another good source for referral. Finally, your states affiliate of the American Psychological Association (APA) will have a list of licensed psychologists in your area.

3. **Residential treatment.** The first two levels of treatment are usually enough to bring about change in children and young teens. However, sometimes a residential treatment setting is required to get a child to learn that there are limits to his behavior or to provide the round-the-clock treatment and structure necessary for some of the more serious problems such as severe depression, schizophrenia, or drug addiction. These settings include hospitals that focus on behavioral health, schools, or even outdoor therapeutic programs where kids live in small groups under professional supervision in structured outdoor environments. Using such a facility is not a snap decision but should be made after serious consultation with other professionals that you have been working with. My main point in bringing this option to your attention is that you need to never give up on your child. The so-called "tough love" approach of kicking a rebellious child out of the house sends the wrong message: that you have given up on your child. A better message might be: "We love you and want to see you grow into a healthy and happy young adult, but either you have to let us be the parents around here—which means we are in control—or for your own health and safety, we will have to find a treatment facility that will take control."

•   **Sports, arts, hobbies, and recreation.** Spirited children need healthy outlets for their CAPPS. Without healthy outlets, these same traits of curiosity, adventurousness, power, persistence, and sensitivity will find outlets that are anything but healthy. Tobacco, alcohol, and other drugs, sexual activity, and even crime are all waiting around the corner to provide the adrenaline thrill that spirited kids often desire. Even young children will get into adventures that drop your jaw in disbelief. Providing your child with opportunities for structured activities not only provides the challenge she wants but offers opportunities that help in the taming process.

Being part of a team, whether a sports team or an arts team, creates the need to cooperate with others and follow the instructions of the coach or leader. Because children are often highly motivated to stay on the team and get more participation time, they usually try harder to learn these lessons. Teams also provide the opportunity to belong to something bigger than oneself. Since all children crave a sense of belonging, being "a Tiger," "in the chorus," or "on the team" helps the child establish ties that lead to taming.

Spirited kids also benefit from being good at something. Maybe your child struggles with schoolwork and finds himself in trouble a lot on that front. Developing a sports skill, musical talent, or other strength can give him a sense of competency that grounds him and boosts his self-esteem. I once asked a young woman who had struggled through childhood and adolescence what helped her make it through and turn out so well. Her reply was, "I sang in the chorus." Not only did she feel good about her talent, but she made friends with others in the chorus who appreciated her gifts and shared her common ground of singing. Being part of a team or developing a skill can do the same for many children. Consider some of the following opportunities that may be available in your community:

- Recreation department athletic leagues
- School sports
- Private lessons, from karate to guitar
- Church or community center leagues

- Extreme sports like biking, rollerblading, rock climbing, and skateboarding
- Choral groups, bands, orchestras, and other musical opportunities
- Scouting or other outdoor-based organizations
- Religious youth groups
- Civic groups for families that stress charitable work together
- Summer camps (either general or built around a particular sport or skill)

At the same time that you encourage these and other healthy activities, keep an eye on how much time your child spends in front of a screen: television, computer, video game, and the like. These activities are usually fine in low doses but can easily become so time consuming that they squeeze out more beneficial group activities. Be sure to set and enforce limits on screen time.

Friends and Relatives

There is an old saying about advice: Consider the source. You're more likely to take advice from someone you regard highly than from someone you barely know, much less from a person with whom you always seem to be arguing. Because parents of spirited children are so often engaged in struggles for power and other conflicts with their children, their words often fall on deaf ears. The same message coming from a favorite aunt, uncle, or even family friend can often get through much more effectively. Maybe you have talked to your child about the importance of doing well in school and getting along with the teachers a thousand times, to no avail. Enlisting the aid of a friend or relative that your child likes and respects to have a similar talk may give your position new credibility. Perhaps your child is refusing to follow your instructions in matters around the house. Again, a heart-to-heart talk with another adult about the importance of cooperating with one's parents may help.

The use of friends and relatives is especially important for single parents. Children benefit from the influence of both sexes, often learning complementary roles and skills from each. When one parent is missing or rarely involved, the child misses out on valuable lessons. In addition, a single parent may find the job of discipline much more difficult without the presence of the other parent for backup and support. In such cases, encouraging a favorite adult to be more involved in your child's life can help fill the void. If you have a sibling who you think would be a good influence on your child, consider asking him or her. A good friend could also fill the role, although I caution against bringing in someone you are dating too early. It is tough on kids if and when a breakup occurs, so it is usually best to wait until the relationship is on very solid footing before involving the significant other in an adult-friend role.

You may also want to consider a mentor for your child. Organizations such as Big Brothers Big Sisters can help you find a good person for this role, or perhaps your religious organization or other agency in your community can help. Back in my single days, I volunteered as a Big Brother to a ten-year-old boy who lived in poverty with his mother and two sisters. He needed a male influence, and I was glad to help. In fact, I got a lot out of the relationship myself, so don't be afraid of imposing on someone. Years later I had the happy honor to be invited to my "little brother's" wedding.

Finally, families have the power to offer children the sense of roots they need to grow strong and healthy. Telling and retelling the special stories of your family's history can ground your spirited child by giving her an understanding that she is part of something large and ongoing. The author Alex Haley demonstrated to millions of people through his book and miniseries *Roots* just how powerful a family history lesson can be. Tell your child about the special stories that make your family both unique in all the world and yet also a part of the larger human family. What country did your family come from originally? What was life like in that country? Why did they leave? What kind of risks did they take in coming to the United States? Who showed courage in starting a new life? What humorous anecdotes capture the spirit of the adventure? How did your grandparents meet? How did you and your child's other parent meet?

As you share your stories, pay attention to what captures your child's imagination. She will want to hear that story over and over again. Encourage her to ask questions, even when you do not know all of the answers. Let her know that you are proud of your heritage and hope that she is as well.

Beyond Taming: Free the Horses

Whatever you do, or dream you can, begin it. Boldness has genius
and power and magic in it.

—Johann Wolfgang von
Goethe (1749–1832),
German playwright, novelist,
and dramatist

IN THE IMAGINARY world of dreams and fiction, somewhere between the lands of Narnia and Middle-earth, not far from the gates to Hogwarts, lies the Kingdom of Arthur. It is here that a strong and capable young teenager named Kelly sets out on a mission to free the king's magical horses that had been imprisoned in a mountain by the evil wizard Zor. Accompanying Kelly on her mission is a menagerie of friends that she meets, Oz-like, along the way. After all, freeing magic horses from evil wizards is too big a job to do alone.

Kelly and her vanguard learn many valuable lessons along the way as they seek the golden spiral of success (made from equal measures of belonging, learning, and contributing) and the three keys to the mountain: lessons about courage and responsibility, cooperation, and friendship, to name a few. They come to understand that "mistakes are for learning" and that "none of us is as smart as all of us," as they overcome one obstacle after another, moving steadily in the direction of their goal.

Finally, as they put the last key into the heavy iron door and watch the magnificent horses dash out upon the beach and gallop away to freedom, they know that they have succeeded in returning hope and spirit to the people of the kingdom. The horses, they have come to learn, are more than mere horses. They are the embodiment of the dreams and talents of the people, without which the kingdom cannot survive.

Dreams and Talents

The above story is part of a twenty-lesson video-based self-esteem and character-development program that I wrote called *Free the Horses.* The program is geared toward children in kindergarten through third grade and attempts, among other goals, to help them learn to believe in their dreams and talents. Dreams and talents are not an idle combination but are critical sides of the same coin called success. I have known too many young adults that lacked one or the other of these vital resources and thus floundered from one meaning-less job to another, never finding fulfillment or meaning. Some had the vision or dream to see something that really mattered to them, but when they went for it, they found that they had not developed the necessary talents to make the dream a reality. I wanted to play profes-sional basketball as a kid but only had enough talent to take me as far as the freshman team at Indiana University. Fortunately, I discovered other dreams along the way, ones that were more closely matched to my talents. I've known others who were incredibly gifted in many talents but had no clear vision of what they wanted to accomplish in life. These people floundered in spite of ability, for lack of a dream. They squandered such gifts as intelligence, charisma, and courage for lack of a clear vision or passion for much of anything.

If you have read this far, you are undeniably committed to taming your child so that he can live a productive life, and you can feel good about the important work of parenting. Throughout this book, I have emphasized that taming is different from breaking in that it strives to preserve the unique spirit that our children have been blessed to possess. This same spirit that drives us crazy contains the seeds of talent and dreams that can help them make a real contribution in the world one day. But taming is not enough. We can establish ties with our child and teach her to live within the reasonable limits of family and community, but this only overcomes the downside of their heightened CAPPS. We want to go beyond this and help them utilize their strong curiosity, adventurousness, power, persistence, and sensitivity to live rich and fulfilling lives. We want to help them learn to nourish their dreams and develop the talents to make those dreams come true. We want to help them free their horses.

Doing these things means going beyond the basic parenting tasks of providing discipline and support. It means finding opportunities to enhance your child's exposure to experiences that can generate passion, imagination, direction, and the development of skills. It means building on their innate curiosity, adventurousness, power, persistence, and sensitivity to encourage the positive, upside potential of these amazing kids.

Beyond Mere Academics: Finding the Passion

Spirited children often run into trouble in school, as their CAPPS get them into trouble with authority. But once tamed, these same traits are not only there to generate school success but to take them well beyond classroom learning into richer, deeper areas. Make no mistake, doing well in school is still incredibly important in opening up opportunities for college admission and then, later, successful and fulfilling careers. And by all means, do whatever you can to help your child succeed academically and behaviorally in the classroom. This includes everything from working with teachers to providing tutorial help as needed. But do not stop at grades. The world is filled with students who made good grades and got into good colleges but who still did not make meaningful lives for themselves.

The people who seem to get the most from their days in school learn to develop real interests in what they are studying. The grade is not the only thing that matters. Stimulating their developing minds and going deeper into areas of academic mystery and adventure become pursuits that kindle a lifelong love of learning. These kids become interested in knowledge, and they find areas in which they are downright passionate. They become the same adults who enjoy reading the paper, a good book, taking an adult education class, and looking up an area of interest on the internet. These are adults who often find careers that do not just give them a paycheck but provide them with meaning and satisfaction. They refuse to believe that "you can't teach an old dog new tricks," as they rise to the challenge of new careers and the learning curves that always go with them.

It has been estimated that the average child today will make five career changes in his or her life. This means that an attitude of lifelong learning will separate those who find the most meaningful careers from those who struggle to find anything. Think about what you can do as a parent to encourage a love of knowledge and learning in your spirited child, building on his natural tendencies of curiosity, adventure, and persistence. Find where his interests lie and see which can be cultivated into passions.

Of course, I'm not talking about a passion for television, video games, and other forms of entertainment. Spirited kids will often gravitate to these areas of easy stimulation, just as they will to soft drinks and dessert if you let them. At the same time that you provide reasonable limits for these activities, be quick to buy books, go to museums, zoos, and aquariums, and otherwise pursue opportunities that can stimulate interest in the world around them. When the spark of interest emerges, be sure to fan it, encouraging further exploration. Ask lots of questions and brainstorm ways for them to go further into their interests.

When Jim's parents realized that their son had an interest in Japanese animation, they were quick to provide opportunities to take him to animation conventions and to learn more about Japan. When Cela's parents saw how excited their daughter was on her first visit to the new aquarium, they surprised her with a small aquarium of her own. Together they searched the internet and read books about sea life as her interest grew into a full-fledged hobby. Once the curiosity of these spirited children caught hold, these parents were wise to provide opportunities to allow their spirited children to explore deeply their areas of interest.

Finding and Developing Talent

Spirited kids have a special need to find their talents in life and build them into horses they can ride fast and far. Their traits of adventure, power, and persistence can propel them to develop skills that others will never reach. Some talents are innate, emerging on their own when the child is exposed to the right opportunity. If your child has special athletic gifts, these will show themselves as she participates in school sports. If he is gifted in an academic subject area, again, there is not much chance of missing this as he moves through school. However, there are many talents that can lie undiscovered because the opportunity never presented itself.

David was a great playground wrestler, but his schools never had a wrestling team, so his talent went undiscovered and eventually was lost. Years later he had the opportunity to watch his son, Sean, excel in wrestling at a school that had a great program in the sport. While you can't provide your child with every opportunity to develop his talents, you can make sure that he is introduced to a wide range of activities while he is young and see where his interests and aptitudes lie. Do not go overboard rushing him from one activity to the next, or you will burn him and yourself out. Just provide him a chance to explore various sports, arts, music, and other areas in moderation. Then when you find one or more that he seems to have a budding passion for developing, begin to allow him to focus more time and attention on this.

I said earlier that some talents are innate. This is the talent of superstars. Michael Jordan, Tiger Woods, John Steinbeck, John Lennon, and others were born with rare gifts that are not available to most of us. They still had to work hard and practice tremendously to achieve the level of excellence that they did, but no amount of practice can create genius. It is either there or it isn't. And genius is not what I'm talking about looking for in your child. I am talking about aptitude and passion. If you set yourself up looking to make your child a superstar, you are both likely to be disappointed. However, while only a very few become superstars, many millions find passion in developing their talents and performing with joy and enthusiasm, whether on the playing field or at the pottery wheel. Help your child develop multiple interests and then put the time into making her become a real talent.

Warren saw that his son Jim was not a gifted athlete, but he had a passion for sports. After realizing that football and basketball were not a good fit for his abilities, Jim got into the sport of lacrosse. He was not particularly gifted on the field, but he found a position that none of the other kids really wanted to play: goalie. He worked hard developing his skills at the position, not just at practice but on weekends with his dad. Warren would spend time with him, taking shots on goal. Jim became quicker and more skilled at the position. By his senior year in high school, Jim had developed his talents so much that he was an all-state lacrosse player helping to lead his team to a state championship.

A side benefit of helping our kids develop interests in the world around them and honing their own talents is that in the process they become more interesting people. Said another way, people who are interested are interesting. They are somehow more alive and vibrant. Their minds are alert. They have things to talk about. And they have a quiet confidence that grows from developing skills and knowing how to develop more of them.

Career Exploration

I admit that I used to frown at adults always asking young children that old question "What do you want to be when you grow up?" I thought that it ignored the fact that what the child was right now was important enough, and we did not need to be pushing them to focus so far down the road. Now, having seen so many young adults who have no direction or passion for anything to do with work, I am reconsidering. Asking young children to imagine fun and exciting careers may very well help them begin to explore the positive side of work, the side that can bring joy and passion to a person's life.

The human desire to make meaning out of one's life is so powerful that those who never find a satisfactory answer to what their life is all about are rarely happy individuals. Of the three main areas for meaning—friendship, love, and work—too many spirited children find themselves unable to solve the problem of work. Maybe the conflicts their spirited temperaments generated throughout school led them to disdain authority, or maybe they just learned to see work as an unpleasant chore that took them away from the real adventures in living. Whatever the reason, parents can help free the natural desire they have to find work that is an adventure in itself.

Use their innate curiosity and adventure seeking to introduce a variety of occupations. Find picture books to read with them when they are young, talking together about the exciting possibilities of different jobs. Share your own satisfactions from work, whether you are a stay-at-home parent or work outside the home. Get them involved in thinking about your work situations as they get older, even asking them for advice as appropriate. Talk positively about work—how good it feels to accomplish something and do a job well. Don't focus on the monetary aspect as much as the meaning that is created by doing something worthwhile and productive with your time. And use your encouragement skills to reinforce their own positive interest and comments about work. As they get older, you might arrange to take them to work with you, or even arrange to swap with other parents so that the kids can experience a variety of occupations. Find time to talk with them about work, asking questions like these to get the conversation going:

- "What jobs do you think would be cool to do when you grow up?"
- "What sounds cool about that job?"
- "What is your favorite subject in school?"
- "What kinds of jobs might be related to that subject?"
- "Would you rather have your own business or work for a company? Why?"
- "Where can we find out about more types of careers?"
- "Why do people work?" (Money, yes, but also stress the satisfaction that people get from accomplishing something useful.)

Community Involvement

Spirited children often find themselves at odds with others, sometimes wanting to overpower others, sometimes being so sensitive to slights by others that they avoid contact. Even when tamed, they can sometimes be so consumed by their own curiosity that they forget to reach out and connect with those most important to them. But to be truly happy, satisfied individuals, spirited children need to feel connected to others. One way to help your child do this is to focus on opportunities to do three things: belong, learn, and contribute. When a child feels a sense of belonging, it gives him a secure base from which to learn. Once he has learned something, he has something to contribute to others. And as he contributes to others, his sense of belonging goes up, leading to more learning and more contributing, in an upward spiral. Possessing these three qualities not only helps a person feel successful but propels him toward actual success.

Encouraging your child to contribute to the well-being of others is not just altruistic; it really helps her become more successful in the process. When people get outside of themselves and feel and do for others, they find an increased sense of satisfaction that promotes their own well-being and success. Charitable giving is also one of our national values. As such, it not only makes your kids better people, it will also put them in good stead with their peers as they get older. Giving and doing for others will also raise their self-esteem and create many meaningful bonding opportunities for your family. To help them develop this lifelong value, try some of the following:

- Talk to your children about your own charitable giving of time and money. Relate what you did and how good it made you feel to do something useful for others.

- Express your positive feelings about others who give. It can be big stuff; for example, "Did you hear that Home Depot cofounder Bernie Marcus gave $250 million to build the Georgia Aquarium? That was really generous of him, and it's something that millions of people will enjoy." It can be little things. For example: "I saw some kids selling lemonade outside their home to help raise money for Hurricane Katrina victims. What a nice thing for them to do!" You can even praise TV or movie characters that give to others. Using such praise is a great way to let your children know what you value, and subtly encourages them to do similar things.

- Give young children money to donate at church or other charitable opportunities, then smile and tell them that they did a good job when they give it. As they get older, discuss an allowance with them and talk about what portion of the allowance should go to charity. Make sure they know that you are giving them money for this purpose and then follow up to make sure the money is given. As always, be sure to offer your encouragement when they give.

- Make it a point to spend family time doing charitable work together. There are lots of organizations that can help you decide what to do. Start with the internet or your religious organization for ideas. Then go as a family and make it enjoyable. Afterward, go out for lunch or dinner and talk about what you accomplished and why it is important to do for others. Try to make this a regularly scheduled activity; say, once a month. Otherwise, you will find that the demands of ordinary living require all of your time, and you'll never get around to this sort of volunteer work.

- When you make a meal or a dish for a family or friend in need, involve the children in the cooking and then let them help you deliver it. Again, keep it fun, and be sure to show your encouragement for their help.

- Have a family talk about why the world is a better place when people help each other. It starts with family members helping each other, expands to helping others in your school and community, and then eventually expands to reaching out to people all over the world. For example, your family might decide to "adopt" a child in another country through one of the fund-raising programs that work to fight child hunger.

• Come up with your own family project by talking together. You might decide to raise money for some worthwhile pet cause or adopt a needy family during the holidays. Involve the kids in the discussion, decision making, planning, and execution.

Broadening Horizons

If I ever doubted that the world I grew up in had changed, it was not the day my son, Ben, announced that he would be studying Chinese in school. When I grew up, China was a lightly regarded country with too many people and the wrong type of government. Besides, all the Chinese restaurants had menus printed in English anyway, so why would anyone want to study Chinese? Now I have no doubt that Ben will one day order a Chinese meal for us in a restaurant in Shanghai.

The Nobel Prize–winning author Alexandr Solzhenitsyn once gave the following advice: "Know people, know places, know languages." As our world continues to become more interconnected, this advice is more applicable than ever before. Spirited children are endowed with a sense of adventure that is a natural fit for a world in which you can fly from Atlanta to Singapore in a single day and email someone there in a click of a key. Help them find ways to experience the depth and breadth of this amazing collection of people, places, and languages. If you can afford to take family vacations beyond your own national borders, you can open up whole new worlds to your children. As they get older, foreign-exchange programs provide reasonably priced opportunities for teens to spend time with families in other countries. Internet pen pals can be another way to go beyond borders and learn about the world.

We made it a policy in our family to alternate trips to the beach or mountains for rest and relaxation with educational/adventure trips to other parts of our own country and abroad. Your kids may not think a trip to historic Boston is as exciting as one to Disney World, but with a little research and some planning, you can find things that everyone enjoys. For us it was a performance of the Blue Man Group—appealing to our son's love of comedy—that helped balance out historic walking tours and drives in the country. If you take the kids abroad, be sure not to over-Americanize it. The idea is to let them experience another culture and to meet people who can broaden their horizons. If you stay at a big American hotel, eat at McDonald's, and run in to see the Mona Lisa before rushing back to the hotel to watch TV, they miss the experience of foreign travel. Be sure to make time to process the experience as you go by asking questions and sharing observations with your children.

To get the most out of travel, involve the children in planning the journey. Go online together, share other resources, and talk about what you would like to do. Making sure that older kids have a camera or access to a family camera is a great way to heighten their sense of observation. When you get home, you can print out the best pictures, make a photo album, and then share memories and observations later as you relive the trip together. Take videos on which family members take turns making commentary about what the family is doing; it's a great way to deepen the experience now and later.

14

Meanwhile, Back at the Corral:
Your Taming Plan in Action

*A thought which does not result in an action is nothing much, and
an action which does not proceed from a thought is nothing at all.*
—GEORGES BERNANOS
(1888–1948), French author

I SUGGESTED IN chapter 3 that you read the entire book before putting any of these ideas into action. The reason I gave was that the information and skills that you would be learning work together as an eight-sided taming corral in which your spirited child might bolt from one side to another. Unless you had all of the skills necessary for these eight planks in mind at once, it would be difficult to know what to do when your child responded to your new approach. On the other hand, keeping an 80,000-word book in mind even after you have read it is a Herculean undertaking. In fact, Hercules, a spirited adult himself, who was prone to fits of rage, would likely have balked at the task before you!

This chapter is meant to help you review the essential methods presented in this book and plan how you will use them with your own child. It is not a substitute for the rest of the book, and trying to use it as such will probably be an exercise in frustration. There is too much information left out, and without the details, it may not even make sense. But if you have gotten this far and are still with me regarding this theory and practice of taming, this chapter should help to strengthen your memory and ability to apply these ideas to your own child. If you want even more help, I suggest that you form a study group with other parents of spirited children and discuss this book chapter by chapter as you support one another in taming your children at home each week. Having an experienced facilitator lead the discussion would be even better. Check the Resources for further information about parent education groups. Now, a quick review of the eight planks forming the sides of our taming corral.

Plank 1. Leadership (chapters 1, 2, 3, and 4)

Concepts

Spirited children need to know that there is a leader or leaders in the family, and that leader is not them. Parents usually err by either being too permissive with their children, in an attempt to avoid power struggles and tantrums, or too harsh, in a misguided attempt to become the child's master and break his or her will. Enlightened parental leadership is both firm and yet respectful. Yes, you are the boss, but a boss who leads with consideration for the child and a genuine caring about his wants and feelings. Problem solving and character development become the goal rather than blind obedience to authority, as the parent strives to prepare the child to maximize his spirited nature while learning to live within the limits of family and society.

Key skills

- Use a firm and friendly tone of voice.
- Do not fight and do not give in to unreasonable demands.
- Hold the reins loosely, but hold the reins.
- Work with your child to find solutions to conflicts, but do not give up your authority to make the final decision.

Plank 2. Prevention (chapters 1, 2, and 10)

Concepts

Understand your child's spirited nature and how her tendency to be more curious, adventurous, powerful, persistent, and sensitive impacts her relationship with others, including you. Recognize the upside of these CAPPS as well as the problem side, and work toward using that knowledge to head off problems before they occur. Learn what triggers her negative reactions and take steps to avoid them. Be particularly aware of what triggers your child's anger, as well as your own anger, and work on ways for you both to become slow to anger. Understand the relationship between outside events and your child's thinking, feeling, and doing in response to these triggers. Then plan how you will use each of these four elements to help reduce tantrums, rage, and other over-the-top expressions of anger.

Key skills

- Identify what triggers your child's negative reactions.
- Talk with your child about anger and plan together some ways to help him stay calm.
- Make sure she gets enough sleep and good nutrition.
- Develop a good metaphor for measuring anger with your child (for example, the stove or the thermometer).
- Teach him to find alternatives when his goals are blocked.
- Use your anger metaphor to help her express her feeling in words, not misbehavior.
- Teach your child how to use 1-4-2 deep breathing to calm down.
- Experiment with the use of water and bathing as a calming technique.
- Agree on a cool place for him to go when he begins to overheat.
- Teach problem solving.

- Set limits on the expression of anger: no destruction, disrespect, or violence.
- Don't fight or give in.

Plank 3. Relationship (chapters 4 and 9)

Concepts

Remember the wisdom of the African healer who taught the stepmother to tame her stepson like she did the mountain lion: slowly and patiently. Find ways to build a friendship with your child, remembering that you do not need to give up your role as authority in the family to do so. Build your relationship on the acronym *FRIEND*—fun, respect, interests, encouragement, no, and delight—as you reawaken the feeling of joy between you and your spirited child.

Key skills

- Play together at least ten minutes every day: board games, sports, computer or video games, roughhousing, creative play, acting, watching TV, movies, or plays together, reading together, laughing together, water play, and more.
- Treat your child with respect, just as you expect him to treat you with respect.
- Know your child's interests and show interest in them.
- Teach your child skills and let her teach you.
- Avoid discouraging acts such as personality attacks, focusing on mistakes, showing a lack of confidence, expecting too much, and valuing your child only for her behavior.
- Learn to encourage by building on strengths, showing confidence, setting realistic goals, and valuing the child for herself.
- Say no when necessary, but avoid hard no's when possible and help the child find acceptable alternatives.
- Find something in your child that delights you!

Plank 4. Power (chapter 5)

Concepts

Understand your child's excessive desire for power and how power struggles work. Recognize that all humans want power and that power is neither good nor bad. Our goal as parents is to help our children learn to use their tremendous power in positive ways. In any power struggle, the person in a position to say no is in the more powerful position. Parents must therefore learn to use creative discipline strategies for getting the child to say yes rather than shows of anger and punishment, or bribes or giving in. The use of force often increases resistance, just as giving in increases the use of force. The result is a push-push power struggle. The way out is to stop pushing without giving in. Solve the problem.

Key skills

- Don't fight and don't give in.
- Give choices, not orders.
- Motivate with when-then scenarios.
- Stay firm and friendly.
- Ask for what you want respectfully.
- Avoid character attacks or other methods designed to hurt or shame the child.
- Take your sail out of your child's wind.
- Put yourself in your child's shoes.
- Acknowledge the legitimacy of your child's wishes (even when she can't have them).
- Do the unexpected.

Plank 5. Structure (chapter 6)

Concepts

Spirited children require discipline in order to learn to live within the limits of civilized society. But the old-school methods of reward and punishment do not work well with modern children. A good first step in providing discipline for your child's spirited nature is to create structures to help him learn to live within limits. These structures operate like corrals, helping a wild horse learn to accept limits to his freedom as the handler works to tame him. Understand that spirited children need a flexible structure. Learn to focus your use of structure on time, space, and behavior.

Key skills

- Buy a kitchen timer if you have children under the age of ten.
- Establish routines for bedtime, mornings, daytime, homework (if your child is in school), dinner, weekends, and holidays.
- Build fun aspects into each routine.
- Involve your child in developing these routines according to age and level of maturity.
- Build in unstructured time and be willing to alter routines as the situation requires.
- Develop structures for the following spaces with your child: her room, a cool place for calming down when she overheats, a study place, and a place to play outdoors.
- Make sure he knows what is off-limits.
- Establish family rules or guidelines of behavior.

Plank 6. Discipline (chapters 7, 8, and 9)

Concepts

Respectful discipline is a useful means for preventing misbehavior and helping children learn from the experience when they do misbehave. Avoid discipline that is too harsh, but do not be afraid to provide discipline as needed. Understand the interaction among discipline, empathy, and problem solving, and use that understanding to teach your child to live within the limits of the situation while getting her needs met at the same time. Do not resort to spanking or other outdated and less effective forms of discipline. Take the time to learn and practice better methods, and work at using them consistently. Remember that discipline alone accomplishes nothing or may in fact backfire, but discipline used in conjunction with the relationship-building skills that establish ties with your child can accomplish quite a lot.

Key skills

- Natural consequences (allowing your child to learn from experience when it is safe).
- Polite requests and gentle reminders (start gently and become firmer as needed).
- Firm reminders.
- "I" Messages: "I have a problem with ____. I feel ____, because ____. I would like you to ____. Will you do that? Great, when?"
- Logical consequences: "Either ____ or ____. You decide." "When you ____, then you may ____."
- The FLAC method: feelings, limits, alternatives, and consequences.
- Family problem-solving meetings.
- Provide encouragement on a regular basis and use the SUGAR method to build positive and successful behavior: small steps; use encouraging words; go for the next step; acknowledge strengths, effort, progress, and successes; repeat as necessary.

Plank 7. Problems (chapter 11)

Concepts

Spirited children are often centered on their own wants and needs and can use help in learning the critical relationship-building quality of empathy. As you teach your child to problem solve, help him learn to identify his own feelings and then the feelings of others. Help him learn to find solutions to problems rather than demanding his own way. Model the give-and-take of cooperative problem solving by helping him solve his problems using effective communication skills.

Key skills

- Learn to listen to what your child is feeling behind his words and actions.
- Use a feeling word to help him learn to label his feelings for himself.
- Avoid "sidewinders" when helping your child solve a problem.
- Teach your child to identify alternative solutions and evaluate possible consequences.
- Use "palms-up" problem solving when your child has a problem: empathy, brainstorming, action, follow up.
- Ask questions that help your child learn to look at others' feelings during conflicts.
- Have regular family meetings.

Plank 8. Resources (chapter 12)

Concepts

Taming a spirited child usually requires the efforts of multiple well-intentioned and capable adults. While parents are the keys to taming, wise parents will seek to utilize the help of various members of the community to help reinforce their message and provide additional lessons for their child. Identify where in your community that help is available. Reach out to the school, spiritual organizations, recreational leagues, health professionals, family and friends, and others as much as possible. Just as you want to filter out negative influences that will mislead your child, look to filter in as many of these positive resources as makes sense.

Key skills

- Identify outside resources in your community that can help you tame your child, particularly: the school, a religious institution, recreation opportunities, friends and relatives, and if necessary, mental health resources.
- Find the best school you can for your child.
- Be an involved parent, working with the school to support your child's learning and behavior.
- Find a loving spiritual outlet for your child's spirited nature, including, if possible, a Sunday school experience and other opportunities for reinforcing moral education.
- Consider whether your child has a learning disorder such as ADHD in addition to his spirited nature; if you think it is likely, have him evaluated by a professional.
- Consider using medication and therapy to help if such a condition exists.
- Get your child involved in one or more of the following: sports, arts, hobbies, and other forms of structured recreation.

- Help your child develop a relationship with an adult friend or relative as a mentor who can reinforce your messages and provide added support and encouragement.

Developing Your Plan of Action

While some of the planks in the taming corral are triggered by your child's behavior, others require you to take the initiative and begin the process of change yourself. Because there is too much to attempt all at once, you will need to phase in these changes gradually over a period of weeks. I suggest that you begin with the relationship-building planks and then gradually add the time, space, and behavior structures from chapter 6. This will require you to be ready with your new discipline skills, as your child will inevitably test to see if you will fight or give in when he bucks against the corral plank. In addition to the discipline skills in chapters 7 and 8, keep the information about power struggles from chapter 5 and the ideas about anger from chapter 10 in mind as well.

The following action plan is an example of how you might proceed. Be sure to modify it to fit your knowledge of your child and the needs of the situation.

Weeks 1 and 2. Relationship Building

Think about the relationship that you have with your child and review chapters 4 and 9 for ways to improve it. Make it a point every day to do these three things: play together, encourage your child, and say "I love you." I repeat, do these three things every day! Then add in other methods of building a relationship, as you think best. Also, during this period, find something about your child that delights you.

Week 3: Begin Building Taming Corrals

Talk with your child about the need for structure. Begin with a bedtime routine and then move on to other times of day. Keep it positive and be sure to build plenty of fun into the routines themselves.

Week 4: Add Corrals for Space and Behavior

Don't make too many rules, and only makes ones that are necessary, but be ready and willing to enforce your rules once made. Encourage your child to help make the rules with you and be sure to let him know which rules apply to adults as well. You will also need to add rules as situations come up. You might say something like, "I think we need a rule for that. What do you think?" Keep your tone friendly, but be firm as necessary.

Week 5: Talk About Anger and Establish a Metaphor for Heating Up

Refer to his cool place that you established in week 4. Teach the 3-12-6 deep-breathing exercise for calming down and see how she likes it. Talk about other self-soothing methods including bathing and other uses of water.

Week 6: Use Palms-Up Problem Solving and Other Empathy-Training Methods from Chapter 11

Look for opportunities to focus on feelings—your child's and other people's—and apply the four steps of palms-up problem solving. Be sure to offer lots of encouragement.

Week 7: Identify Outside Resources and Make Sure That Your Child Is Involved in At Least One Sport or Arts Activity

Review chapter 12 and find resources that you can use to provide healthy outlets for your child's spirited nature and to provide you additional support in helping in the taming process.

As you put your taming plan into action, remember to be patient and encouraging with yourself, as well as with your children. Avoid getting discouraged if progress is slow or if your child backslides. That's to be expected sometimes. You may backslide as well. Under stress, people often revert to earlier learning, so there is no way to accomplish your goals without some mistakes. Better be ready to catch yourself with a smile instead of a kick, correct yourself when you can, learn, and move on. Use the SUGAR recipe on yourself: *s*mall steps; *u*se encouraging words; *g*o for the next step; *a*cknowledge strengths, effort, progress and successes; *r*epeat as necessary. Reread sections of this book from time to time to help you remember what to do, get the support of others, and stick with it. You'll find the results worth the effort.

Conclusion

The fox gazed at the little prince for a long time.

"Please—tame me!" he said.

"I want to, very much," the little prince replied. "But I have not much time. I have friends to discover, and a great many things to understand."

"One only understands the things that one tames," said the fox.

THE ART OF taming a spirited child requires time. It cannot be done overnight, and it cannot be done without committing effort and energy to the process. But the payoff comes from knowing that you have made a huge contribution to your child—and to every person that child will come in contact with throughout the rest of his life! The payoff also comes in the deepened understanding that emerges from your relationship with your child. "One only understands the things that one tames." Allowing your child to stay wild not only does a disservice to him and others, it robs you of the true joy of parenthood; that of really understanding your child and what makes him the special person he is.

Understanding means seeing your child at a feeling level, well beyond the behavior and misbehavior that characterize so much of parent-child relationships. Learning to listen for your child's inner voice that tells about his fears and hurts that lie beneath the sound and fury of his anger. Picking up on the bits of pride she feels as she masters a difficult task or learns to manage her temper. These feelings aren't available to the normal senses of sight and sound. They require you to listen with that part of your parental intuition called heart. As the fox taught the little prince, "It is only with the heart that one can see rightly. What is essential is invisible to the eye." Learn to listen to your child with your heart and then respond with your heart, your knowledge, and your parenting skills, and you will connect at a level that creates the tie that tames.

Resources

David and Claudia Arp. *Answering the 8 Cries of the Spirited Child*. West Monroe, LA: Howard Publishing Company, 2003.

Lindsey Biel and Nancy Peske. *Raising a Sensory Smart Child*. New York: Penguin Books, 2005.

Michele Borba. *No More Misbehavin'*. San Francisco: Jossey-Bass, 2003.

Kristi Meisenbach Boylan. *Born to Be Wild: Freeing the Spirit of the Hyperactive Child*. New York: Berkley Publishing Group, 2003.

Sam Goldstein, Robert Brooks, and Sharon K. Weiss. *Angry Children, Worried Parents*. Plantation, FL: Specialty Press, 2004.

George T. Lynn and Joanne Barrie Lynn. *Genius! Nurturing the Spirit of the Wild, Odd, and Oppositional Child*. Tucson: ChildSpirit Publications with Hats Off Books, 2004.

Michael H. Popkin. *Active Parenting Now*. Atlanta: Active Parenting Publishers, 2002.

————. *Active Parenting of Teens*. Atlanta: Active Parenting Publishers, 1998.

Gail Reichlin and Carolyn Winkler. *The Pocket Parent*. New York: Workman Publishing Company, 2001.

Antoine de Saint-Exupéry. *The Little Prince*. Orlando: Harcourt Brace Jovanovich, 1943.

Mary Sheedy Kurcinka. *Raising Your Spirited Child*. New York: HarperCollins Publishers, 1991.

Daniel J. Siegel and Mary Hartzell. *Parenting from the Inside Out*. New York: Penguin Group, 2003.

RESOURCES

Rita Sommers-Flanagan and John Sommers-Flanagan. *Problem Child or Quirky Kid?* Minneapolis: Free Spirit Press, 2002.

John F. Taylor. *From Defiance to Cooperation*. New York: Three Rivers Press, 2001.

For more information on these and other related parenting resources or to find a parenting group in your area visit www.activeparenting.com.

Acknowledgments

My intention in writing this book was to help the parents of spirited children reframe the way they look at these amazing children and at the same time to provide concrete skills for bringing out the best in them.

I have wanted to write this book from the first time I gave a seminar called "Taming the Powerful Child," some thirty years ago at a Montessori school in the Virgin Islands. (I know, but somebody had to go!) My ideas on the subject, grounded in the psychological theory of such historical giants as Alfred Adler, Rudolf Dreikurs, and others, have been developing ever since. But alas, I got busy writing and publishing other books and videos about parenting and my "taming" book remained in a file in back of other files. My thanks go to my literary agent, Scott Mendel, who sought me out after reading one of my works and subsequently teased this book out of my memory. Without his initiative and guidance it might still be on my "to do" list of good intentions.

I also want to thank both Oprah Winfrey and Montel Williams for repeatedly having me on their respective shows. The subject of each of my most recent visits with them involved parenting children who were quite spirited and dealing with parental anger as well as child misbehavior. My guest appearances pushed me to think more critically about this area of parenting and triggered many of the ideas—and some of the examples—in this book. I also acknowledge the wonderful contribution each of these superstars has made to parent education through their broadcasts. Their commitment to families gives television a good name.

In preparing for one of my appearances on these shows I came across Mary Sheedy Kurcinka's wonderful book *Raising Your Spirited Child*. Although the term "spirited" has been used to describe a certain type of person for centuries and much has been written about that type of person and the "spirited child," Ms. Kurcinka is the first to my knowledge to attempt to give the term "spirited child" a clear behavioral description, identifying between five and nine specific characteristics common to such children. My own experience with such children and their parents over the past thirty years often parallels her observations, and we have both identified two traits these children share—persistence and sensitivity. However, the two traits that I have found are the most troublesome to these children and their parents are their adventurousness and *power*. The anger, fear, and intense power struggles engendered by these traits make it paramount that parents learn ways to handle them effectively. I have attempted in this book to do that, while also explaining my "taming" philosophy for handling all of the traits of spirited children. Nevertheless, my own writing about these energetic children is informed by Ms. Kurcinka's ideas, and I appreciate her contribution to the field of parent education. If you have not read her book, I highly recommend it.

I thank both my editors at Simon & Schuster—Trish Grader, who graciously inherited my book, and Nancy Hancock, who first signed it up—for your confidence in this book and for your suggestions and guidance during the editing process. My thanks is also due their assistants, Meghan Stevenson and Sarah Peach, for your work in bringing the manuscript to publication, to Philip Bashe for your excellent copyediting, and to Lisa Healy for making sure production was on time and done well. Finally, my gratitude to Debbie Model,

Marcia Burch, and Jessica Napp for your creativity, hard work, and experience in bringing me together with the reader.

To my wife and parenting partner, Melody Popkin, thank you for modeling that vital combination of strength and love that all spirited children need from their parents. Our son, Ben, is better for it. And so is this book. And finally, to Ben, I appreciate your willingness to let me use examples from our family life to help illuminate ideas in this book . . . but not as much as I appreciate your own wonderful spirit.

Index

INDEX

ABOUT THE AUTHOR

MICHAEL H. POPKIN, PH.D., pioneered the field of video-based parent education with the introduction of the *Active Parenting Discussion Program* in 1983. Since then he has authored and produced more than thirty books and videos, including *Active Parenting Now*, *Active Parenting of Teens*, and *1, 2, 3, 4 Parents!*, which have been used around the world to teach millions of parents how to raise happy and successful children. A frequent keynote speaker and media guest, he has appeared on more than two hundred television shows including multiple appearances on *The Oprah Winfrey Show*, *Montel Williams*, PBS, and as a regular parenting expert on CNN. A former child and family therapist, Dr. Popkin received his Ph.D. in counseling psychology from Georgia State University. President of Active Parenting Publishers *(www.activeparenting.com)*, he lives in the Atlanta area with his wife and teenage son and misses his daughter, who is away at college.